BREAKING OUT *of the*

"MAN BOX"

THE NEXT GENERATION OF MANHOOD

TONY PORTER
COFOUNDER OF A CALL TO MEN

Skyhorse Publishing

PRAISE FOR
BREAKING OUT OF THE "MAN BOX"

"Tony is a man of great character and virtue, a leader in the charge to end domestic violence. It has been an honor to fight that battle alongside him. With *Breaking Out of the "Man Box"* Tony has taken the extra step to offer organic solutions to cement a culture change to end domestic violence using the illustration of the "man box." His book challenges us all to be better men, not just bystanders, but in pursuit of doing the right thing."

—Troy Vincent, executive vice president, NFL Football Operations

"Breaking Out of the "Man Box" is a powerful look at manhood and its connection to violence against women. This transformative read is for fathers, sons, husbands, brothers and friends—for any man who wants to create a world where all men and boys are loving and respectful and all women and girls are valued and safe. Readers will want to be part of the Next Generation of Manhood."

—James Brown, network broadcaster, CBS Sports and CBS News

"A life-changing read for the well-meaning man. *Breaking Out of the "Man Box"* heightens readers' awareness of their potential impact on women in their lives and communities, and lays a bold foundation for preventing violence against all women and girls."

—Peter Buffet, copresident, NoVo Foundation

"Tony Porter's book is a well-meaning man's call to other well-meaning men to end the silence, ask difficult questions of ourselves and those around us, and begin a unified discussion that will lead to a lasting, meaningful solution."

—Danny Pino, actor, NBC's *Law & Order: SVU*

In loving memory of
my mother, Marie Nelson Porter,
who lived her life with the trauma of sexual violence.
She hid the injuries from her children
in hope that our pain would be lessened.

Skyhorse Publishing books may be purchased in bulk at special discounts for sales promotion, corporate gifts, fundraising, or educational purposes. Special editions can also be created to specifications. For details, contact the Special Sales Department, Skyhorse Publishing, 307 West 36th Street, 11th Floor, New York, NY 10018 or info@skyhorsepublishing.com.

Skyhorse® and Skyhorse Publishing® are registered trademarks of Skyhorse Publishing, Inc.®, a Delaware corporation.

Visit our website at www.skyhorsepublishing.com.

10 9 8 7 6 5 4 3 2 1

Library of Congress Cataloging-in-Publication Data is available on file.

Cover design by Brian Peterson
Cover photo credit: Leroy Harden

ISBN: 978-1-5107-6184-1
Ebook ISBN: 978-1-5107-0149-6

Printed in United States of America

Contents

Introduction

People are taken aback by the idea of men standing up and speaking out to end violence against women and girls. Within the socialization of manhood, tradition teaches men to have a lack of interest in women outside of those they love and care for. So for men to speak out publicly on behalf of women and girls is outside of the norms that define manhood. I have thought about this question a lot: How did I come to do this kind of work? While I would like to say that I simply woke up one morning and decided to do the "right" thing, that's not the case at all. The truth of the matter is that women have inspired me at different points in my life and continue to inspire me about my role and responsibility as a man.

People often ask me: "Why do you work with men to end violence against women and girls? Did something happen to you as a child? Was your father abusive? Were you abusive? Were you molested as a child? The answer to all of these questions is "no." It is important for me to mention that my mother was sexually abused by my grandfather throughout her adolescent years, though she did not share this with me until I was already doing this work.

While I spent many years challenging our social constructs as they relate to racism and other forms of group oppression, I had given little attention to sexism. I worked in a small community in New York, just north of the Bronx. Women in that community were paying close attention, dedicating their lives to addressing male domination and its role in domestic violence and sexual assault. Women in that community and others I knew in and around New York State took an interest in my development. I must admit I was a difficult subject matter at times. It took many women in and around my life over a period of years, challenging my thoughts on manhood, to wake me up. We shared many years of thought-provoking, meaningful conversations and subsequent self-reflection. These and countless other women invested time, energy, and wisdom, eventually influencing my thinking about the collective socialization of manhood. In this process as a man I felt like a student, and I guess, there was so much to learn. It was difficult at times to understand and accept the role I played in marginalizing and dominating women. As good men—because we don't physically abuse women or intentionally do anything to harm them—it can be difficult to understand the role we play in supporting a culture of male violence toward them. At times I was resistant to the teachings; this is common behavior with members of any dominating group—whether it be race, class, or others. But I continued to engage in these conversations and women remained patient with me, and eventually I understood why it was important for men to take a stand—to end violence against women and girls, and to promote healthy and respectful manhood.

This book is a call for men to hold on to the wonderful things about being a man, like the pride we take in working hard, being providers, and loving husbands, partners, and fathers, while examining some aspects of manhood that are tripping us up. We need to reexamine the aspects of manhood that are not benefiting our well-being and that support a culture of violence against women and girls.

The motivation to write this book, along with reasons of equity and humanity, includes my need to celebrate the life of my mother, Marie Nelson-Porter. Because of her, and the wonderful relationship she had with my sisters, I was privileged from an early age to see that women are incredibly courageous and special. I cannot explain it all but I do know that the best of me comes from my mother and her influence. My mother passed away on the evening of March 15, 2000. On that day, I made the decision that I would spend the rest of my life celebrating her life. I dedicate this book to her memory.

Steeped in the socialization of manhood is the need to be in control.

Good Men, It's Time to Be Part of the Solution!

At this point, you may be questioning why you picked up this book in the first place. You are a good guy, not one of those men who would ever put his hands on a woman. You would never commit rape or hit your wife or girlfriend in a fit of anger or rage. In fact, you would threaten physical harm to any man who abused a female loved one of yours. In your opinion, you are not the problem, so how does this book have anything to do with you?

Well, this book has *everything* to do with you.

You are a well-meaning man who can help to end violence against women and girls by being a part of the solution. A well-meaning man is one who believes that women should be respected—especially his wife or girlfriend, mother and daughters. Often referred to as a "good" guy, a well-meaning man wants women to be treated fairly and thinks that abusing a woman in any way is unacceptable.

Well, it's time for those of us who are "good" men to acknowledge the role male privilege and socialization play in domestic violence, teen dating violence, sexual assault, sex trafficking, as well as

1

in aggression against women in general. It's time for us to claim collective responsibility. It's time for us to become part of the solution.

My intention in this book is not to bash any good man. I know that an assault on men is not going to end the assault on women. Instead, through a process of reeducation, I seek to help us understand how we play a part in this problem. Unfortunately, despite all the goodness of the well-meaning men, we have been socialized to operate in a system where our role includes domination, dehumanization, and oppression over women. This can happen in such small and insidious ways that we're unaware of it. And it's sometimes so easy and accepted to behave this way that we don't question ourselves about it.

Now please do not think I am claiming to be perfect or have it all together. I am still a work in progress as a well-meaning man. Before engaging in the work of ending violence against women and girls, I never considered myself to be sexist at all. When I found myself in situations where women were challenging me on what they defined to be my sexism, I was extremely insulted. I would often think and sometimes say to myself, *They don't know me. They don't know what they're talking about. I am not sexist.* But, these women would not let me off the hook that easily.

During this time I was a fairly well-known trainer around New York State on addiction studies. I trained addiction professionals and students on a variety of topics related to better serving chemically dependent people. Many of our training efforts focused on issues of race and class, urban and suburban, and we explored various ethnic groups as well. The goal was to understand what was required to best serve them. When it came to addressing "women's issues," I did not make the same effort as I did with issues of race and class.

So, with a lot of love and patience, women in my circle helped me to understand that I could not effectively teach about racism without understanding the impact it had specifically on women of color. Similarly, I could not effectively teach about classism without an in-depth understanding of the experiences of financially poor women. What are specific challenges when working with financially poor women of color that are different from financially poor men of color? With all these topics, I knew I had a lot to learn. It was time for me to challenge my own personal teaching about manhood in order to truly understand the experiences of women in a male-dominating society.

Over the next five years, I immersed myself in learning about sexism and male domination. I began to understand and develop a critical analysis of the collective socialization of manhood. This is when I really started to recognize that domestic violence, sexual assault, and all forms of violence against women are rooted in a sexist, male-dominating society.

I began to cultivate the skill of talking to men about our role and responsibility in ending violence against women. I understood the challenge ahead of me. I quickly learned and understood that as men we have been collectively taught to define what it means to be a man by distancing ourselves from the experiences of women. In order to effectively distance ourselves we are collectively taught to have a lack of interest in women and girls outside of those we love. This is not saying that we are bad or uncaring men; I know it might sound that way. Nor does it say that we as men are all in the same place with this thinking. It does say though that we are all aware of this collective teaching. When exploring the collective teaching of manhood I have found that the more we as men and boys express an interest in the experiences of women and girls, outside of sexual conquest, the more our "manhood" may come into question. It should be noted that our collective understanding of manhood is extremely heterosexist and homophobic. Further, this collective socialization of manhood teaches men to see less value in women, to view them as the property of men and as objects, particularly sexual objects.

So the toughest question became: how do I engage men in order to discuss these historic barriers already in place? And how do I accomplish that in a loving, respectful, yet accountable way? Luckily, in my favor, I have always been the kind of man that other men respected, and I always give respect right back. So, rarely have I been in situations with men where I am outright disrespected. I would learn to perfect this skill as I engaged more and more men about breaking out of the man box.

I understood that as a man it was important for me to "meet men where they are," and not expect them to instinctively have a high sense of consciousness when thinking about these issues. I recognized that I could love men through the process even when I strongly disagreed with their thoughts and views. I learned that I could hold men accountable for inappropriate language and behavior during our engagement in a loving way. My goal is to draw men into my message, not put them on the defensive and create more distance. One of the ways I learned to engage men is through the experiences of women they love and care about. My motto became: Reach in and grab the hearts of men, ensure that they leave your presence thinking and feeling differently than they did when they entered.

THE IMPORTANCE OF TRANSPARENCY

A key skill and requirement I learned for engaging men is transparency. Steeped in the socialization of manhood is the need to be in control. The opposite of control is vulnerability, which is a feeling not acceptable and far outside of the man box. So what I had come to know is that if I want men to talk about and share their experiences, which means asking them to be vulnerable, I would in turn have to do the same. Not only would I have to do the same, meaning share in a vulnerable way, but I would have to do it first. Over a period of time, by sharing *my* life stories with men, I learned more about my socialization to manhood in countless ways.

I began to relive times and experiences throughout my life, with a new lens. I was able to make sense of experiences that had previously baffled me.

I think back to my own father and an example of the impact male socialization had on his life. My brother, Henry, had died tragically when he was a teenager. The burial was a two-hour drive outside of New York City on Long Island. It was a sad, horribly sad, day. As we were preparing to come back home from the burial, the limousine stopped at a restroom to let folks take care of themselves before the long ride back to the city. My mother and my sisters all got out, but my father and I stayed in the limousine. As soon as the women left, he burst out crying. I was twenty-one years old and had never seen my father cry before. He didn't want to cry in front of me, but he knew he wasn't going to make it back to the city without letting out his feelings, and I guess he thought he was better off allowing himself to express those feelings and emotions in front of me rather than in front of the women. This was a man who ten minutes before had just put his teenage son in the ground. That's a grief I can't even imagine. The thought that sticks with me the most is that he began apologizing to me for crying in front of me and, at the same time, he was also giving me props and lifting me up for not crying.

I have come to look at this as a perfect example of the socialization of manhood. The fear of publicly displaying emotions other than anger—this fear has us paralyzed and is holding us hostage. We have been taught as men that showing and sharing emotions is a sign of weakness. We have been taught that men are strong and women are weak. We then go about our business rarely ever showing emotions other than anger, and never displaying weakness even when we are in the grip of it. So much of what we have learned about what it means to be a man is defined by distancing ourselves from what we perceive to be the experiences of women. This process of distancing ourselves requires that we also develop a lack of interest in the experiences of women. This lack of interest is central to a culture of violence.

As men we have been taught that domestic violence, sexual assault, and other forms of violence against women and girls is a women's issue, resulting in us spending very little time, if any, addressing it. We explore this issue from a male-dominated perspective, at times leaving little room to hold ourselves and other men accountable. Fortunately, most men do not intend to hurt women, and many have no idea that their behavior supports men who are violent. Most men are just going with the flow, doing things as they have always done. Operating from this place of domination leaves little room to account for the reality of how we affect women and how they experience us. Our limited willingness to empathize with the plight of women adds to the problem. Moreover, we tend not to listen to them, which is key to understanding how sexism and male domination manifests.

As men, far too many of us don't listen to women enough. Instead, we justify our conscious and unconscious ability to tune them out by saying that women talk too much, nag, and so on. So it should not be a surprise that many men don't want to hear what women have to say about issues related to domestic violence and sexual assault. Speaking from my personal experience, taking direction from women and actually listening intently to what they have to say could actually expedite the process of ending violence against women and girls (while promoting healthy and respectful manhood) in the United States. Women have been asking men to listen for years and it's time that we do.

At the end of the day, what we are addressing is the issue of humanity. We are attempting to move away from the gender binary roles that define us. I have a vision of this huge space called "humanity" where everyone can just be themselves, as well as loving, safe, and valued. I have to believe that it is women's leadership that will help us create the levels of humanity so many of us crave.

We are still at a place where most of our efforts to end men's violence against women are being led by women. At the large majority of places that I go to speak, I am invited by women to speak to men. This book, in fact, will more likely be purchased by women and given to the men instead of individual men seeing the book and being intrigued enough to purchase it. Further, women will know when they take the book to their husband, their boyfriend, their son, their dad, their brother, or their coworker that they need to say, "Hey, read this book. It's an easy book to read. Look at it. It's not that long. I think you will enjoy it." They have to preface it in that way; otherwise it's likely the man won't read it.

My hope is that as men read this book they will begin to understand and examine male socialization. Consider that even as well-meaning men we create, normalize, and maintain a culture that supports violence against women and girls. Understand that while there are many wonderful things about being a man, we are still a work in progress.

My desire is for men to think about their position as well-meaning men and how we prefer to separate ourselves from men who assault and abuse women. We make monsters out of them as a means of supporting our position that we are vastly different. Likely, we remain focused on the need to provide some type of treatment for them—pathologizing their violence, blaming family history, chemical dependency, mental illness, or an inability to manage anger.

But ironically, for the most part, in my work I have discovered that these are not the reasons men abuse women. Nevertheless, we focus on the aforementioned reasons because it further distances us (well-meaning men) from the "bad" guys, strengthening our status as "good" guys. In doing so, we squeeze out the space needed to understand and acknowledge that violence against women and girls is a manifestation of sexism and male domination. Once we can come to admit that sexism plays a part, we will also see that all men are part of the problem.

Men who abuse receive permission to behave this way from those of us who are well-meaning men. We give permission in several ways; we stay quiet and are inclined to mind our own business. Often, we do not get involved where domestic violence is concerned because we have been taught that women are the property of men—a "she belongs to him" perspective. For this reason, our silence is permission and diminishes the likelihood of creating a culture where men hold each other accountable.

Okay, I know some of you may be thinking, *slow down, you're hitting me with too much too fast.* No worries, in this book we will walk through this step-by-step together. I will share with you many of my personal experiences, as well as what I have learned from them. This book grew partly out of a series of discussions I have had with men over the last ten years. These men are of various ages, ethnicities, and have different levels of education and family backgrounds. What do they all have in common? They were all well-meaning men. Probably a lot like you.

In the world that I envision for my daughters and yours, and how I want men to act and behave, I need you on board. I need you with me. I need you working with me and me working with you on how we raise our boys, teaching them to be men. We can show our boys that it's okay to not be dominating. That it's okay to have feelings and emotions. That it's okay to promote equality. That it's okay to have a woman who you are *just friends* with and that's it. That it's okay to be a whole person. That our liberation as men is tied to their liberation as women.

So as you read this book, I invite you to examine your own role as a well-meaning man in our society. Likewise, I encourage you to challenge other well-meaning men to join you. Together, we can create a world where all men and boys are loving and respectful and all women and girls are valued and safe. This is long overdue. It's time to get started.

The collective socialization of manhood, also known as the man box, is what men and boys are taught it means to be a man.

Lessons of the Man Box
Women Are of Less Value

The collective socialization of manhood, also known as the man box, is what men and boys are taught it means to be a man. Most men are good men, just operating on remote control—doing things the way we always have, the way they were taught to us. Most men are not aware that the teachings and actions of the man box help support and provide the fertile ground for a culture of men's and boys' violence against women and girls. By deconstructing and unpacking the man box we can get a better understanding of its impact. As we challenge those notions that have a direct impact on the well-being of women and girls, let's also keep in mind that there are many wonderful things about being a man: We love the women and children in our lives, we are hard workers, coaches, and mentors. For the most part we live our daily lives simply trying to do the right thing and take care of those we love and are responsible for.

This teaching defines manhood by distancing boys from the experiences of women. The man box teaches boys to have less value in the experiences of girls. The man box teaches that men are strong and women are weak. It teaches that women are too emotional. The man box teaches that men are in charge and in control. It teaches boys to have no fear and to not acknowledge pain, particularly emotional pain. It teaches that men are the protectors and that they rarely ask for help. Asking for help is viewed as a sign of weakness.

The man box teaches that women are the property of men and are objects, particularly sexual objects. Young men are taught to have a limited interest in the experiences of young women beyond sexual conquest.

The man box is also extremely homophobic and heterosexist. It is my belief that homophobia and heterosexism are the glue that keeps the man box together. Let's examine many of my own personal experiences to deepen our understanding of how this collective socialization operates in our day-to-day lives.

I was born in Harlem, New York; soon afterward we moved to the Bronx. My father was a numbers runner, and he also had a couple of "after-hours spots" where people could buy booze when the liquor stores and bars were closed. In our community, he was what we called a Hustler, making an "honest" day's living, not hurting anyone, just doing his thing.

Moving to the Bronx was a big thing back then. It was sort of like the theme song on the television show *The Jeffersons*, we were "movin' on up." We lived in a five-story walk-up apartment. Over the years, the Bronx neighborhood changed, and crime and drugs became a part of the normal flow of things in my community. In the building next to mine lived a guy named Johnny. When I met him, I was about twelve and Johnny was about sixteen. Johnny liked to hang out with all of us younger guys, and parents from the neighborhood always wondered, *why is that older kid hanging out with those younger kids?*

Our parents had good reason to be concerned about us hanging out with Johnny because most of the time he was up to no good. His father was not around and his mother had died from a drug overdose. Johnny was being raised by his grandmother who worked two jobs to make ends meet. So most of the time, Johnny was unsupervised, roaming around the neighborhood doing exactly what he wanted to do when he wanted to do it. On this particular day, I was out in front of the house playing when Johnny looked out his window and called me upstairs to the fifth floor where he lived. I did not hesitate. When Johnny calls, you go. We younger guys all looked up to him. He was smooth, cool, handsome, and had a way with the girls. He was even having sex. So, when I got up to his apartment and he asked if I wanted "some," I knew exactly what he was talking about. According to my socialization as a boy, even at that age, I was supposed to know. Johnny did not have to explain or elaborate, nor did I ask any questions because I knew what he meant. Johnny was referring to sex.

Time seemed to stand still following Johnny's question, as many things ran through my mind at once. Right at that very moment, my growing reputation in the neighborhood was at stake. Based on how I handled this situation, my reputation could be severely tarnished or, at the least, set back a bit with the need to redeem myself. Mind you, my friends could be cruel; redemption could be a very slow process. Understand that I already knew what kind of young man I wanted to be and how I wanted others to perceive me. I certainly wanted to be liked and respected by my peer group and adults as well. I wanted to be able to hang out with all types of guys in the neighborhood: good guys, athletes, musicians, and even the "wanna be" gangsters from time to time. I could actually jeopardize my fate by giving the wrong answer to this one question. There was too much riding on it. I desperately needed to get it right. Telling Johnny the truth, which was that I had never had sex (and was not ready to) was not an option—wrong answer.

Among boys, it is very rare to openly admit or volunteer that you have never had sex. In fact, if you are brave enough to let that truth part your lips, it is often to your closest friend, who is then sworn to secrecy for life. So as boys, we act almost as if there is no first time. Though virtually impossible, we act like we have been having sex since the age of two. I guess I could have told Johnny that I just did not want to have sex at the time, but somehow I knew that would be a wrong answer too. I aspired to be a "real" man (often thinking that I already was) and everyone knows that "real" men don't turn down sex. We are supposed to want it all of the time and never, ever say no. We are taught that boys or men who refuse an opportunity to have sex will likely have their manhood questioned. Instantly, you'd be asked if you are gay, assumed to be gay, or called gay to your face. And the truth of the matter is we would not use the term gay, instead, every derogatory and dehumanizing name to describe gay men would be in play. Homophobia and heterosexism both ran deep in my neighborhood. I certainly could not leave myself open to that, which left me only one choice. When Johnny asked, "Do you want some?" my answer was "yes."

Next, Johnny told me to go into his room and I did. On his bed was a girl from the neighborhood. For our purposes, we will call her Sheila. Everybody knew that something was a little strange about Sheila. She was mentally ill or developmentally delayed. Of course I am professional and mature right now, but at that time, mentally ill or developmentally delayed was not a part of my peers' vocabulary. As boys we generally used a host of inappropriate names to describe Sheila: dummy, idiot, retard, and more. She was nude and Johnny had just finished raping her, though he would have called it having sex because she did not say no.

Naturally, Sheila didn't say no due to her mental capacity, but she never said yes either. Back then such an act was not considered rape, thankfully today it is. Lack of consent includes the incapacity to give consent. Consent means indicating "yes" by words or clear decisive actions. Anyhow, I closed the bedroom door and leaned my back against it, hoping Johnny wouldn't come right in behind me and see the look of terror on my face. I was petrified. My fear had nothing to do with having sex. I had no intention of doing anything with, or to, Sheila. My main concern and fear was how to save face with Johnny. I was not concerned about what was happening to Sheila. Remorsefully, I admit that I did not value Sheila or have any feelings about her reality because I really had no connection to her. I lacked interest in her and believed she had very little value. The reality is that if she had a brother, father, or crazy uncle who was respected in the community, she could have gained value through them. She did not have a man to give her value. Based on my understanding of manhood at that time there was no reason for me to feel obligated to stand up for her. Protecting Sheila was not my responsibility. This situation felt like it was all about me, and safeguarding my growing reputation.

The point here is that many men take the position of minding their own business. Our socialization absolves us from responsibility for women whom we don't know. Consider the difference well-meaning men could make if they actually made the safety of all women their business. Since Sheila's well-being was not my issue, my main concern was me and my budding reputation, which could have been easily derailed if Johnny found out that I was afraid to have sex with Sheila (which would have been rape). So, as I stood there trying to figure out what to do, it occurred to me that I had been in the room long enough to have done something and my time was running out. I needed to figure out how I was now going to get out of his room, emerging as *the man* or at least *a* man for the time being. Then instinctively, in my twelve years of wisdom, I unzipped my pants and walked out into the living room with a fabricated swagger, hoping to convince Johnny that I *handled my business*. When I entered the living room, it resembled the waiting room of a doctor's office. There was an audience of about five guys sitting there who all happened to be friends of mine. While I was in the bedroom, Johnny had gone back to the window to call them up for their turn to get "some."

All of them seemed so eager to gang rape Sheila, though they definitely could not see the wrong in what they were doing. They just called it having sex, *knocking boots*, *running a train*, or *getting some*. Deep inside I knew it was wrong, terribly wrong, but all the teachings of the man box outweighed any sense of morals or injustice.

During a training not long ago, with male participants from the age of sixteen to about seventy, I asked the question of the older men what was it called when you were a teenager and boys lined up to have "sex" with one girl. The men said it was called *running a train*. I then asked the same question to the sixteen-year-olds and they said it's called *running a whore train*. What this tells me is that for at least three generations there has been limited growth in our collective socialization of manhood regarding the objectification of women.

So my friend asked, "How was it?" I began to head for the door. I turned and responded, "It was good," and then I zipped my pants up in front of them and walked out. They bought it and I had survived the test. I don't know exactly what happened to Sheila after I left. I figured since I did not actually participate or harm her in any way, that I was okay. I was certainly not a "bad" guy.

However, the truth of the matter is I was just as responsible as Johnny and the other boys. While I could not physically stop them from doing what they were planning to do to Sheila, I could have told someone. Yet, that never crossed my mind. Or, perhaps I could have simply just told Johnny how I felt it was not right to take advantage of Sheila. Deep inside, I knew that she could not defend herself and she was at the mercy of all those boys. But, I never said a word.

Surely Johnny thought I approved of the whole episode because I didn't express otherwise. My silence gave him permission, as if what he was doing was acceptable to me. It's this line of thinking, the kind of teaching and socialization, that implies, "If I don't participate, then I'm okay," which followed me throughout a good portion of my life. I know this thinking follows most men. Considering that attitude, well-meaning men are not likely to intervene on behalf of women being abused, especially if they do not know them. Minding our own business is commonplace. Thus, violence against women will continue until we make it our business. And making it our business does not always mean physical confrontation. For men that's usually our first thought. Making it our business *can* include calling the authorities when needed, challenging the thinking of other men, rethinking what we teach our sons and other boys, and how we model behavior with the women in our lives.

It's about five years later. I'm sixteen or seventeen still living in the same community, having grown up with the same set of friends. I had achieved the reputation I was seeking. I had a girl-friend and everything in my life was going smooth. I was a decent young man, no problems with school or the law, respected by adults and peers alike. A decent athlete and musician, I was able to move in and out of different circles of people. Many things had changed from the days when I was a younger boy running around the neighborhood, or so I thought. The reality was some things were still the same. I can recall the day that felt like déjà vu to me. I was on my way into the place we called the "spot," which was merely a clubhouse in the basement of the building I lived in, but we were too cool to call it that. As I entered, I could see a line of my friends, about five or six of them leading up to the boiler room door. When I saw them, I immediately knew what was going on. This time around I had some status in the neigh-borhood and felt way more comfortable voicing my opinion. I stormed past my friends, expressing along the way that what they were doing was not cool. They sort of blew me off and held their place in line as if I hadn't said a thing. When I pushed into the boiler room, there she was just as I expected. It was Sheila. She was on an old mattress in the corner pushed up against the wall. My friend had just finished getting "some," or should I say taking "some" because what he had really done was raped her. I know that he would have said he was having sex with her because she never said no, but note that she never said yes either.

I looked at my friend as he pulled up his pants, and I said a few choice words to communicate my disapproval and then I walked out. The other guys could hear me and as I passed them on my way out, there was a heated exchange with them as well. Nevertheless, I left them to continue what they were doing, and I exited the "spot."

When I share this story, people often ask me how I felt about what was happening to Sheila. The fact is that I think about Sheila more now than I did at the time. Back then, it was about me and I didn't have a lot of feelings about Sheila's world or her reality, even though I knew what they were doing was terribly wrong. What troubled me later was that I did so little even the second time I saw Sheila in that horrible situation. Unlike the previous time when I was younger, I could have done something to help Sheila—I should have maybe helped her up, gotten her dressed, or walked her out. None of my friends would have tried to stop me. I could have even told them that this behavior must stop or maybe influenced them to stop. Instead, I did nothing.

When I think back on this time in my life, I recall that I did feel bad for Sheila. The problem is that I never felt responsible for what did or did not happen to her in my presence. Neither was anyone holding me accountable for not standing up to my friends. I stayed true to the collective socialization of manhood, which assured my innocence as long as I did not participate in the deplorable behavior.

I still thought I was a "good" guy, and so did everyone else as far as I could tell. However, how could I be totally blameless when I tolerated this behavior from my friends?

I am sorry to say that I was a part of a brotherhood of men and boys, connected in a way that allowed its members to get away with inappropriate and criminal behavior with little, if any, consequences.

In fact, with regard to women, the male culture that I am speaking of allowed me to keep my "membership" as long as I respected certain women, like my family or the family of my friends. For the most part, other women didn't really matter and tended to be free game. This is where we can start to see the relationship that well-meaning men have with abusive men.

Although well-meaning men do not necessarily give the go-ahead for abusers to act, they do adhere to a set of unspoken rules, which imply approval. The set of standards, expectations, and rules that regulate our behavior, thoughts, and ideas are confined to the man box.

The man box dictates how we act; moreover, it reinforces specific beliefs and opinions regarding women. The man box also defines manhood in a way that rewards those who are true to its tenets while chastising those who fall short. The male codes have been passed down from generation to generation. Breaking down the man box and social norms will ultimately help well-meaning men identify and hopefully rectify the behavior.

Consider athletics as a primary example of where you can see the man box at work. Back in the day, I spent many afternoons and nights on the basketball courts of New York City. We called it street ball, and we played it with a lot of vigor and much attitude—bring your "A" game baby. "B" games are not welcome! We would definitely let you know if your game or skills were not up to standards. Street ball was about aggression, power, and strength. Fancy or slick moves would not make it too far. If a guy came down the middle, in the paint with one of those *dippa dee doo* moves, the next thing he would remember was being helped up off the ground.

I am ashamed to mention the ways we would intimidate others into believing that they shouldn't even be on the court, but I am sure you can imagine. The names we used to tell a man his game was not up to standard included all the derogatory and dehumanizing terms associated with women or gay men.

Keep in mind that I am a "good" guy, a well-meaning man, but my man box had taught me that lack of athleticism meant a guy was soft, of less value—like a girl or a woman.

It took me some time to make the connection between what I was doing, thinking, and saying and the relationship my behavior had to violence against women. I was simply following the rules and teachings of the man box. Keep in mind that every time I would say to a man, "You're playing like a girl," I was really saying that women are less capable, less significant compared to men. Now perhaps our makeup as men does give us a physical advantage in some cases. However, the point to focus on here is the mindset that is continuously reinforced and then transferred to other areas, which is that women are "less than" men. You tell a boy he is playing or doing anything like a girl and he immediately attempts to change that dynamic. He has been socialized by the age of five, some say as early as three, to know that's a place he does not want to be . . . associated with a girl or women. We criticize boys who have a close relationship with their mothers by calling them a "mama's boy"; obviously this is interpreted as a negative. When that same boy is hanging out with his dad, he is referred to as "a road dog" or "a hang-out partner," "best buddy," and so on, all positive. Recently at a gathering I heard a three-year-old tell his mother, "You can't come with us, only for me and daddy." I know this sounds innocent and it very well may be, but what are the subtle messages he is already receiving about women?

Men should act like men, according to the man box, by living up to the expectations that we have among each other or risk being called a chump, sissy, punk, or worse—a girl. Think about how this must make women feel and also what this says about how men feel about women in general.

Well-meaning men knowingly or unknowingly support the teaching of the man box in many ways, including how we differentiate our sons from our daughters with regards to parenting. A man will tell his son to stop crying, while telling his daughter that she can cry as long as needed, or more likely make no comment to stop her from crying, thus implying it's okay to continue crying. A man will tell his son to stand up straight and tall, to stick his chest out and hold his head up, but tell his daughter to put her head on his shoulder and relax because daddy will take care of everything. A well-meaning man will tell his son that he is the man of the house and he needs to help take care of things, as he tells his daughter that she is "daddy's little girl" and he will take care of her.

We teach our sons to be tough, strong, and to take charge, yet we are the exact opposite with our daughters by telling them to make peace, be gentle, and try to get along with everyone. Rarely are men and women treated equally as adults in society, and I challenge you to think about how early this socialization begins.

The socialization process begins immediately—day one. I speak from experience; my youngest two children are my son Kendell and daughter Jade. Kendell is fifteen months older than his sister. Today, I can see the impact my socialization has had on all of my children, particularly my sons. My journey of transformation happened during the raising of my two youngest children, and I can share extensively my experience. But while I have gained tremendous insight and my fathering skills have enhanced greatly, breaking out of the man box continues to be a challenge. Fortunately, I am now more aware of my challenges related to male socialization, and I hope that you will be too after reading this book.

Male socialization, even as a parent, suggests that I should love (unconditionally), pamper, cuddle, spoil, and protect my Jade at all costs. While there is nothing wrong with this, the man box teaches it is not acceptable to treat Kendell the same way. I remember some experiences raising Kendell that speak to the challenges the man box presents to parenting skills. Not very surprising, but I have found these experiences to be extremely common when speaking to fathers about parenting their sons.

When Kendell was five years old and Jade four, she would come to me crying about whatever, climb on my knee, and cry it out. Many times I would not even ask her what she was crying about, the most important thing was that Daddy was going to take care of her. Now on the other hand, if it was Kendell crying, the moment I would hear him crying it was like a clock would go off, an immediate countdown would begin. In fact, he had about thirty seconds of crying maximum. The truth of the matter was his time was up once he reached me. Unlike Jade, I wouldn't lift him up and put him on my knee, instead I would say things like, "Stop crying, hold your head up," "Look at me, I can't understand you when you're crying," "Boys don't cry," etc. And of course the more I yelled and challenged him the more he cried.

Out of my own frustration and fear that I was not raising him to be respected by other boys and men, I would find myself saying things like, "Just go in your room now! And get yourself together, and then come back and talk to me, when you can talk to me like a man!" The boy was just five years old. I'm both remorseful and ashamed of this story and the experience and impact it had on my son, who by the way is a happy, healthy seventeen-year-old young man today. It is important for me to share my transgressions with men in hope that they can see themselves in my story and rewrite their own.

When I told Kendell to "get yourself together," I learned later through conversations with men, that is code language for "in control." The man box teaches men that they must always be "in control"; the opposite, "out of control," is reserved for the experiences of women. As stated earlier, manhood in many respects is defined by distancing oneself from the perceived experiences of women.

What's also in play is teaching boys to stuff away their emotions. From speaking with men, it has been determined the average age a boy is taught that it's no longer okay to cry in public is about five years old. That is the approximate age when we begin to cut feelings and emotions off in our sons and other boys. It is not expected that they will immediately stop crying in public, but this is when the developmental process begins. The expectation is that by the time they are ten years old they will have perfected it. Based on our current definitions of manhood, if a ten-year-old boy still cries on a regular basis in public he is open to being teased, harassed, and bullied.

Now on the other hand there is no particular age when it becomes unacceptable for girls or women to cry in public. While I am told by women that there are times, professionally speaking, when it would be frowned on, in general it's acceptable to cry and share and show emotions when needed.

Speaking of crying in public, one notable manifestation of the man box comes to mind that happened when Kendell was eight years old and started playing tackle football. On this particular day the man box was in full swing—football, men, fathers, and sons all in one place. Kendell was playing football in the Pop Warner League, which has very strict weight limits. Kendell was a big boy, too heavy to play with the other eight-year-olds. Today, at seventeen, he is six foot four inches tall, two hundred fifty pounds, size fifteen shoes and all muscle. He is a big, strong young man and was a big, strong boy with no weight to lose. This meant he had to be bumped up a division and had to play with the nine-, ten-, and eleven-year-olds.

Taking cues from the man box, Kendell did not want anyone but the coach to know how old he was, for fear that the other kids would critique his game and blame it on his age. He wanted to prove he could play with the big dogs and hold his own.

The season was about two-thirds over and Kendell was the starting center on the team and doing a great job. He was doing such a good job that the coach began giving him some playing time at linebacker position. Now linebacker on defense in football is a premier position—you have to be strong and fast. You're required to make touchdown-saving tackles. You're in on about 50 percent of all the tackles. I was a proud dad when I saw him practicing in the linebacker position and couldn't wait for the next game. Go Kendell!

So on this particular day the man box was in full swing, the boys were on the field practicing football, and the fathers were off to the side, discussing sports of course. The mothers were on the opposite side of the field talking "women stuff" and the young girls were having cheerleading practice off in the distance. It can't get any more man box than that.

Anyway, Kendell is playing right linebacker and doing okay, holding his own. The last play before the practice ends, a running back comes out of the backfield with the ball. Kendell goes to tackle him and he takes Kendell for a ride about ten yards down the field before they go down. In football this is called "getting trucked," like being run over by a truck; and, not to put it lightly, Kendell got Mack trucked! The rest of the defense was also on the chase, and they all ended up piling on top of the running back. Guess who was at the bottom of that pile? My son Kendell.

Now remember I was off to the side talking with the dads and other men, though I saw everything that just took place. But, per the teachings of the man box, I could not just end my conversation with the men abruptly and run over to see if Kendell was hurt. Instead, I pretended I was paying attention to the conversation with the men, as I watched, from the corner of my eye, the pile unravel to make sure that Kendell was okay.

In hindsight, I am sure that some of the dads were also inconspicuously watching the pile unravel, acting as if they were listening too. But, they were probably thinking to themselves, *Man, his son just got trucked!* I've come to learn that men do a lot of pretending, one upping and even lying, always trying to keep up with the demands of the expectations of the man box, especially in front of each other.

I wanted the other dads to at least think that my son was tough and could take a licking, so I could not seem alarmed or overly concerned. I just kept a poker face and continued with the conversation. Eventually, Kendell got up and he was moving kind of slow, but he appeared to be okay. After that play the coach brings all the boys together and they talk for a while. Ten minutes later, the practice is over and Kendell and I start walking toward our truck. As we get closer to the truck, his shoulders start to slump over and by the time we reach the truck, he burst out crying. The conversation went something like this:

"Kendell, what's wrong?"

"I'm hurt."

"You're hurt?"

"Yeah, I'm hurt."

"You're hurt?"

"Yes, I'm hurt! Didn't you see what happened over there?!"

"Yeah, I saw it, but that was ten minutes ago. Why are you crying now?"

"I couldn't cry in front of them."

"So, you have been holding it in for ten minutes?"

"Yeah. I had to…."

Deep down, I was glad that he did not cry in front of his peers because he may never have lived it down. Truth of the matter, I was looking around as we were having this conversation to make sure none of the other boys or fathers saw my son crying. On the other hand, I felt horrible that he felt pain and could not let it out. I knew that he, directly or indirectly, got the teachings of the man box reinforced by me that crying in public was unacceptable. I began to wonder where I got that same message from and then I thought back to my father.

I thought about my brother dying tragically and my father's struggles sharing his emotions. That day, my father had desperately tried to hold back his tears and some thirty years later, his grandson Kendell was doing the same thing. When I talk to other men and ask how many of them have never seen their fathers cry, usually two-thirds of the men raise their hands. Conversely, when I ask if there was ever a reason to cry, based on what they knew their fathers had been though, all of the men raise their hands, saying, "many times."

So men, why is it okay for our daughters to be emotional, to cry, to be cuddled and held, but it is not okay for our sons? Male socialization teaches that crying and expressing emotions is something that women and girls do, that it's a sign of weakness. The man box teaches that crying and expressing emotions is also a violation of our defined manhood. While there are acceptable moments, for the most part, we emphatically express disapproval when seeing men and boys cry. This is our way of holding other men accountable to the norms of the man box.

These notions of manhood support a belief system that women, because they are more likely to cry and show emotions, are somehow inadequate, of less value in comparison to men. It is important to note that men could learn something from women in this case because they live an average of ten to fifteen years longer than men.

I remember when Kendell had his first fistfight and lost; it was with a kid from the neighborhood. It was a hot summer day and he was about five or six at the time. He ran into the house crying, I mean falling out, snot-running-out-his-nose crying. Other than being emotional from feeling terribly hurt, there was no sign of physical injury. I must admit that I almost lost my mind for a few minutes. Actually, I was furious. I thought, *How could this be happening? Maybe I should have been teaching him how to handle himself better.* Actually, I hadn't thought there was any need to teach him how to fight, as he was just five or six years old. My other thought, which I am ashamed to admit, included going out to slap the other kid around myself. Even though I would never do this, it did cross my mind.

Next, I considered knocking the kid's father out, because the reality was we didn't particularly care for each other anyway. I knew I could take him, which was very important to the man box. But I don't live this way; therefore, I knew I could not do this. So, I got out the telephone book. I was going to send Kendell to karate school, and then I also had the bright idea of setting up a gym in the basement to teach Kendell how to box. As you can see, I was losing it.

The whole time my wife Tammy was watching me with this puzzled look on her face. The look was a combination of confusion and disgust, so she finally said, "Why don't you just take Kendell to the boy's house and let them make up and be friends?"

This was a novel idea to me because where I grew up you only did that if you won the fight, not if you lost. Plus, you were supposed to be thinking about revenge, not making friends.

At the time, I could not envision myself taking my son by the hand, in tears, and with snot running down his nose, over to this other kid's house for him to apologize and make up. That would start Kendell off wrong—outside of the man box. Moreover, I would be just as guilty for breaking the man box code by encouraging him to go over and apologize because I am his father. I wanted to protect my son and I thought I was doing so by insisting that he be tough.

With the growing knowledge I had regarding male socialization, the man box still overpowered my intellect in this situation. Children should have the freedom to express themselves authentically without adults directing them to live up to our predisposed gender expectations because they will carry those ideals into adulthood. If I had it to do over again, I would simply hold my son and tell him that everything would be okay, plus encourage him to be the bigger person and make peace with his friend. I would also allow him to cry and be emotional and then discuss appropriate options and interventions for the future.

Men, we must begin to understand that we promote less value in women by believing and teaching each other and boys that outward expressions of emotions are what women do and those expressions are of less value. Men and boys will often over-compensate to ensure that they separate themselves from being associated with the perceived experiences of women and girls. This is very problematic because it contributes to an atmosphere that says women are worth less than men, so whatever you do, don't be like them. It also creates the space for men to think that their status in society gives them license to be violent and oppressive toward women. This environment is perpetuated by the man box and cultivated by all men, abusers and well-meaning men alike. No one gets a pass.

THE MYTH OF WOMEN AS PROPERTY

Let us take a look at the ways in which well-meaning men continue to perpetuate the myth that women are the "property" of their husbands, boyfriends, and partners. One of the principal reasons that domestic violence continues to be seen in many of our communities as a private issue is rooted in the belief that men can do as they please with what (or who) belongs to them. While we know this is not literal, many men continue to think this way.

Take, for example, the traditional wedding ceremony, which is a primary illustration of a property exchange between men. We all know it as the father "giving the bride away." The father walks his daughter down the aisle and literally hands his daughter to another man. The woman loses her last name and assumes the name of her new husband through a legal transaction, which seals the deal and completes the ritual or transaction. It's almost like transferring the title of a car when you buy it from an individual seller. The name is changed on the title, to make it legal—just as the woman has her title (name) changed to show that she now belongs to this man.

We understand that this is a figurative part of the ceremony and the exchange of property is not literal; nevertheless, its place in tradition has some relevance. The bride goes from being the responsibility of the father to the responsibility of her new husband, from one man to another. This exhibits male socialization through a very common, cultural practice that supports the idea of women as property. Notice that we are not addressing abusers as we talk about women being the possession of a man; this social thinking is part of the teaching of manhood in general. Many men still accept this traditional practice as a norm, seeing nothing at all wrong with it, that's just how it works.

THE MALL SCENARIOS

When working with men, one of the exercises I use is called "The Mall." I have facilitated this exercise with thousands of men of all ages and cultural groups around the country. There are two scenarios to the exercise. The first scenario is a simple one: A man (you) is at the food court in the mall sitting alone eating. About one hundred feet away another man and woman (assumed to be a couple) are sitting and eating together. All of a sudden, there is a loud sound, like a slap. The man who is alone (you) looks in the direction of the sound and sees the woman crying. The man is standing over the woman in an aggressive manner and the assumption is that he just hit her.

At this point, I pose the question: As a male bystander, what would you do? Many men tell me that they would not likely do anything, but maybe watch to see what happened next or call security if need be. In addition, I often hear men say that they would mind their own business, particularly because they do not know what she did, why he hit her, or the details of the situation.

After collecting these kinds of responses, I change the scenario to give it a different spin. In the second scenario, a man (you) is at the food court sitting alone eating. About one hundred feet away is a woman who is eating alone. A man enters the food court (he appears disheveled) and is going from table to table asking people for money. All of a sudden, there is a loud sound, just like before. The bystander (you) looks over to see this man, the one that was going from table to table asking for money, standing over the woman in a hostile manner and the woman is crying. Again, the assumption is that he hit her. Then I ask the question: What would you do? Here, the reaction is quite different, as most men express that they would definitely get involved. Nearly all of the men say they'd want to "take care" of the man and could not "let this go."

When considering how to respond to the aforementioned scenarios, the determining factor for the men in the exercise is whether the woman was believed to be alone or with the man who hit her. The men were able to admit that they chose not to act in certain situations because of the presumption that the woman "belongs" to the man.

From my observation, this revelation only comes after they hear and compare both situations. Take into account our collective socialization, which leads us to mind our own business, allowing the man in the first scenario to handle "his" woman, his "business." However, it is that same thinking that makes us feel responsible for an unattached female. My experience with men and this exercise shows that when a woman is alone and assaulted by a man who is assumed to be a stranger, men have a higher sense of responsibility and are more inclined to act. This is because we know that there is no connection between the woman and the stranger; moreover, she does not belong to him, so it is our duty to act, much like we are taught to help a damsel in distress.

In the first scenario, we know that the woman does not literally belong to him, but the concept of property is entrenched in our socialization; therefore, we act in a way that indicates that it is okay for a man to have power and control over the woman in his life. When we see this in play, well-meaning men allow it to continue because the man is perceived to be within his rights. Consider the different reactions in both scenarios as the foundation which provides abusive men the space to batter their wives, girlfriends, and partners.

The link between women as property and violence against women comes from the fact that both abusers and well-meaning men think that women are a possession, even if it is only in their subconscious. Most men stay true to this code among men. However, things would be drastically different if well-meaning men would step out of the man box and hold other men accountable for how they treat women, regardless if the woman involved is in a relationship with the man or not.

When speaking with women about the two scenarios, they agreed that the response from men would increase if a stranger were assaulting the woman. But, what they also noted is that they did not believe it would be a substantial increase. Unfortunately they felt, for the most part, that men would mind their own business whether the women was assaulted by her husband, boyfriend, or a stranger.

I am not encouraging men to be violent with other men, but I am advocating for intervention, which can come in many forms. Men have to hold each other accountable, regardless of whether we know the woman and, especially, if we know the man. Men must openly express constant and consistent disapproval. We need to know our local resources, call law enforcement on known abusers, and mentor young men to reverse some deep-rooted issues within the man box that teach that women are the property of men. The main point is that the "good" guys, well-meaning men, have a part to play. If we stand by and do nothing, violence against women will persist. If we continue to stand by and do nothing we are part of the problem and not part of the solution.

As men we have been on remote control.

Property and Sexual Objects
The Collective Socialization of Manhood

In our male-dominated society, objectification of women is commonplace. Breaking down and analyzing objectification and the idea of women as property explains how men come to view women as being of less value. These ideas come from the man box where our socialization leads us to believe that the primary purpose of women (objects) is to support, serve, comfort, satisfy, and entertain men. We often place more value on a woman with more desirable physical features than we do on a woman with high-quality, intangible characteristics.

We should think critically about how we look at women and also how we use them to relax, relieve stress, and entertain ourselves as if they are commodities. Women have more to offer, despite what we have been trained to think and the constant messages we receive from pop culture and other social cues. Whether in the music and entertainment industry, corporate America, communities of faith, or on the street corner, women are treated by men as objects or mere body parts. This has become widely accepted and embraced by mainstream society. For instance, magazines, music videos, advertisements, and commercials exploit women and their bodies. Those images we see on a daily basis condition us to see body parts instead of human beings with opinions, emotions, thoughts, and ideas. Also, take a look at fashion trends for women. Mini-skirts, low-rise jeans, thongs (that show), push-up bras, halter tops, tight-fitting clothing, etc. are all meant to bring more attention to women's body parts. Ironically, you can often find replicas in children's clothing stores as well. In some of these stores you can purchase pants for a two-year-old girl with sayings like "cutie pie" or "honey" embroidered across the buttocks. Here we have clothing, supposedly suitable for an adult woman, made for a child. This goes to show how early body parts become the focal point on the body of a female. Also, keep in mind that the driving force behind many of these companies is a man, most likely a well-meaning man.

It is my belief that, like many other things in the United States, the concept of what is considered physically attractive originated with white men. There is a tremendous pressure on women to conform to this definition, as they assess themselves and try to adjust accordingly. At one time, a slender, white-skinned woman with blonde hair, blue eyes, who was tall (but not too tall), and had medium-sized buttocks and breasts was regarded as beautiful. While today there are many variations of physical attractiveness for women, we still lean in that direction from time to time.

Cosmetic surgeons, makeup artists, and cosmetologists are employed to improve a woman's outward appearance, so that she can compete with other women and meet the standard for attractiveness and appeal to men. On occasion, women have disagreed with me on this point by expressing that they do not visit the salon or wear makeup for men, but instead they do it for themselves. I most certainly respect their views. However, many other women have stated the opposite. They tell me, after contemplation, that they do it to please men.

Fortunately, society has evolved to some degree, as many of the norms established by men with reference to beauty are now more broad and inclusive—with a bold and energetic movement within the LGBT and gender-nonconforming communities adding to the inclusiveness. But what has not changed is the popularity reserved for women who conform.

Think about that woman who is rather conservative; she wears loose-fitting clothes so that you cannot see the shape of her body, does not show any cleavage or skin, chooses not to wear makeup, and keeps her hair in a modest style. Many men would call her plain and probably would not give her much attention. In fact, well-meaning men around the country have told me that they would likely isolate and make her invisible. Not because they want to be rude or mean but because she does not hold their attention.

Perhaps the conservative woman who plays down her sexuality feels liberated. Yet, there is a price for this freedom. Success in dating or meeting a husband or partner, and even securing a job, may be a challenge given the overwhelming investment in the objectification of women. The collective socialization of manhood teaches men, good and abusive, to consider a woman's body parts before her humanity.

I can recall a time while living in upstate New York. In one corner of the yard, I would store some items that I was not quite ready to get rid of yet. In the pile were things like an old 14-foot Jon boat, lumber, bricks, and other junk. I could always count on Kendell to end up playing in that pile, having no interest in the open space that was much safer for him. The problem for my son then was his tendency to fall. Thus, he had scarred up knees and elbows. I used to tease him by blaming his clumsiness on the fact that his body was so slim, but his head was so big. I would tell him, "Kendell, you live on the ground." We would both laugh about it. His scars really didn't seem to bother either of us much. In fact, the man box teaches that men and scars are actually a good thing. Scars and wounds would mark Kendell as a warrior, brave and courageous, a real man. Conversely, the thought of my daughter having permanent scars scared me to death.

My daughter Jade followed Kendell around much of the time, as younger siblings do. But I was constantly telling her to stop mimicking Kendell because I did not want her to fall, hurt herself, or get scratched up like her brother. I remember the day I actually noticed that Jade was catching up to Kendell with the number of marks on her arms and legs. Despite all of my knowledge around sexism and objectification, my immediate thoughts had to do with her as a young woman and how unattractive she would be with those scarred up legs. I had broken my own daughter down into body parts, thinking of her appeal to men and how I should protect her from decreasing her chance to be considered attractive. This shows us how our male socialization is very deep-rooted, a challenge to undo even for men who are conscious of it. As it turns out, Jade has become a skilled softball player; she still loves to play in the dirt, slide into bases, and dive for balls. I love it.

While sitting in church one Sunday morning, Kendell started talking to some girls in the pew behind us. At first, there was nothing alarming about the situation since he was friendly with most of the kids in the church. But, what gave me cause for concern was the look in his eyes and the weird smile on his face as he focused on one particular girl. It took me a while to figure it out. I remembered hearing Jade teasing him just the other day, chanting, "Kendell likes Beatrice. Kendell likes Beatrice," over and over again. It dawned on me, the day had come and it was unfolding right before my eyes. My son had crossed over from thinking girls were gross to being in awe and all sheepish around them. My wife Tammy and I noticed the change in Kendell's behavior at the same time and she urged me to have "the talk" with Kendell. I said to her, "What talk, the boy is six years old."

Of course, there is nothing wrong with boys liking girls, or girls liking boys, but what happens next is what scared me the most. Kendell was only six at that time, but my brain went into fast forward mode because I knew that the man box would soon be in full effect. He could go from having that innocent, boyish crush at six years old, fast forward ten years and he's now sixteen years old. He's standing in the school cafeteria with a bunch of his friends, when a new girl to the school, whom he hasn't met, walks by the group. He then says to his friends things like, "I want to hit that," "I want a piece of that," or "Man, I'd like to tear that (expletive) up."

Now I am and have always been very thoughtful about how I explain things to Kendell. I spend a great deal of time explaining and discussing with him the issues associated with manhood. But nevertheless with all that being said he is still influenced by other men and boys around him as well. Although I am a good father and I try to teach Kendell all the right things, over the years and still today I leave him to the supervision of other men in different capacities every day, from teachers to coaches, youth ministers, etc. Let's face it, he also has a group of friends who all appear to be nice young men but have also been influenced by men.

When working with boys and young men I regularly inform them that most of what they know about being a man they learned from me, that I represent the generation of men that has come before them. That their foundation in what it means to be a man they have learned from us. While they may put a twenty-first-century spin on things, what they know about being a man, I taught them. And the truth of the matter is while I have taught them some wonderful things about being a man, there are some aspects of manhood that we have to rethink.

Well-meaning men teach boys and young men how to think, act, behave, and also how to treat women. I cannot shield Kendell from all those messages, which is why men should be more cognizant of what they say and do around young people. Our young men are watching and picking up man box messages along the way, whether it is in the schoolyard, classroom, basketball court, or other common places. Teachers, coaches, church members, Cub Scout leaders, uncles, men from the neighborhood, and others need to be socially responsible and realize the influence they have on the development of boys and young men in reference to how they view women, ourselves, and life in general.

FRESH MEAT

I am passionate about my work for many reasons and one is my hope that the world will be a better place for my youngest daughter, Jade. She is a young, bright, energetic, athletic teenager. I advise men all the time to envision the world they would want to see for their daughters and other girls that they love and care about. It's an interesting thought for most men to process. I usually follow that statement with a question: In that world, how do you want to see men acting and behaving? The immediate response from men is "respectful." As they think about the question more I began to get responses such as: caring, nice, treat them equal, and so on. It is then that I say to the men, "Our responses to this question speak to the areas where we as men know we are falling short and could be doing much better."

Working with colleges and universities around the country, somewhere along the line, I began to hear the term "fresh meat." It took me back to my high school and college days, as well as back to the neighborhood when a new girl would move in. This definitely applied to first-year female students entering the college. So now I'm working with young men in college and I'm hearing the term "fresh meat." I began the process of having critical conversations with young men from all levels of sports—youth league to professional—and all ages, from high school, college, and beyond.

When I asked these young men to deconstruct the term "fresh meat," the responses ranged from "new," "vulnerable," or "pure" to "untouched" in the virgin sense of the word. They even said, "She may not be a virgin, but at least no one here has hit it yet." I would also get responses such as "sexual object" or "something to be consumed and conquered."

Then I asked these very same young men to fast forward twenty-five years and their daughters are sitting in this same room and we are having a conversation about "fresh meat." This question usually promotes silence in the room. The young men who were chuckling just a minute earlier and having lively, side-bar conversations become silent. You can hear a pin drop. These young men, in this moment, transition mentally from young college men to fathers, and they immediately begin to process and view this issue differently.

The term "fresh meat" takes on a different meaning to them. Why? Well, for one, this might be the first time these young men had a group conversation challenging this aspect of the collective socialization of manhood, truly looking into the future and the world they would want to see for their daughters—and whether or not they are helping to create that world. As men we have been on remote control. Just doing things the way they have always been done without increasing our social conscience or critical thinking. So thinking of a woman in dehumanizing ways would not trigger an adverse reaction. But make that woman their daughter and the reaction increases one hundred fold immediately.

This is why men have to start peeling back the layers of the man box and think more critically. It's only after men consider their own daughters on the receiving end of a term like "fresh meat" that our views, comments, and responses change. Then, none of the "new," "pure," or other dehumanizing adjectives are used. Suddenly, the previous responses don't sound like they are describing a human being . . . because none of the previous responses are what we would want for our daughters.

The sad reality is that we as men quickly become aware that our socialization does not teach our sons and other boys to look out for women against male predators on college campuses. We become acutely aware that she is on her own. We as a result attempt to arm her with all of our knowledge of young men's behavior, their slick and inappropriate moves, the way they may attempt to manipulate her, and so on. Due to the way we have been socialized as men, none of us can depend on any other man to intervene, and to do the righteous thing when it comes to our daughters. It's a sad reality for us to process as men when thinking of our daughters. The truth of the matter is that women have been well aware of this reality and living with it all along.

My second-oldest daughter, Michelle (now grown up), is a graduate of Fordham University in the Bronx. Some years ago, a female colleague of mine used Michelle as an example when trying to get me to understand a point when I was in denial about my own sexism. We were discussing the objectification of women when I stated, "I don't stare at women. I just take a little peep every now and then." You know how sometimes you are about to say something that you know is stupid, but you can't pull it back in time. It's like your mouth is moving just a little faster than your brain; as the words are coming out of your mouth, you're thinking, *Stop! No! Don't say that!* Yet, your mouth is doing its own thing. Well, this was one of those moments. My colleague looked at me with disgust and then started to break it down for me. She called it, "A Day in the Life of Michelle."

Michelle used to commute by bus and train from the Bronx to Manhattan each morning for school and work. As a working, first-year college student, her time was split between the predominantly male real estate company where she was employed and the college campus. Given Michelle's busy schedule and commute—her time on the train, walk from the train to the office and then back, time at work, and the classes she took on campus—my colleague had me consider the number of men Michelle encountered on a daily basis. Based on her experienced estimation, my colleague believed that approximately 20 to 25 percent of the men did what I claimed to do, which was "just take a peep." Other reactions to Michelle would run the gamut over the course of a day. The men would go from just looking and smiling to staring and undressing her with their eyes. Or, some factions of men would say "hello" while others would say "hey baby." Then, there was the more inappropriate group of men who would actually shout out a sexually explicit comment. My colleague also gave me a parting point to ponder at the end of our conversation. She said, " . . . and you know, Tony, most of the men who objectify Michelle are those we define as well-meaning men, and they are probably closer to your age than hers." Putting my own daughter in that space definitely intensified my perspective.

For the most part, the objectification of women is a collective practice of men. We have to take a good, long look at how we have been socialized to treat women as objects. An object is a thing, not a person. Moreover, adding devaluation and thinking of women as property is a lethal combination, which creates a foundation from which violence against women and girls is built on. Regrettably, it's not only my daughter who experiences this reality; it's the daughters, wives, mothers, sisters, aunts, grandmothers, partners, and other beloved women in the lives of well-meaning men. Try asking a woman you know about her day-to-day experience with men and objectification. Men may be surprised about what they will hear; however, men should also take into account how they are possibly doing the same things to other woman. I remember asking a woman friend, "Why don't women talk more about the things that random men do and say?" Her response was, "Men can't handle it." When I really think about her answer, she is probably right. Just imagine your wife, girlfriend, or partner coming home from work; you are relaxing, watching a baseball game and she tells you about some guy down the block who was staring at her buttocks. So you get up, turn off the game, and go outside to deal with this guy. After all, he is looking at your woman. Let's say you get into a little scuffle, win, and go back into the house feeling proud of yourself for defending your wife's honor. Then, the next day she comes home and tells you the same thing. Again, you put down the remote and go outside to deal with the situation. You win again, but this time you limp home. By the time the third day rolls around, most men would be praying that their wives, girlfriends, or partners don't tell them about anything else because of what they would be compelled to do. Women know this and they protect us from each other. They understand that male bravado of the man box would not allow for a peaceful resolution in most cases. Women keep many of these experiences to themselves for the safety of their partners, and in many cases to protect his notions of manhood. Furthermore, women have told me that if they were going to tell us about *all* of their experiences in reference to men and objectification, some of our best friends would be included.

When my son Kendell was twelve years old he was cutting the grass in front of the house. I was on my way home, about ten minutes from the house, when I got a phone call from him asking if he could go down the hill to Sharon's house, a girl from his school. Kendell explained that a bunch of kids from his school were at Sharon's house and he wanted to go down and hang out. I told him that he could go but he had to finish cutting the grass first; he agreed.

As I mentioned, I was only ten minutes away from the house when he called, so as I pulled into the driveway I saw Kendell standing at the lawnmower with about six of his friends. I looked at him and he looked at me.

"What's up?" I asked him.

He said to me, "I don't know Dad, they just came up the hill."

"You know you're cutting this grass."

"I know Dad, I got it, cool out."

I said to him, "I'm gonna cool out alright, you better get this grass cut."

I then waved to all the kids and went inside the house.

What I have not mentioned is that all six of his friends were girls. I'm going to pause in sharing this story and let that sink in: Yes, *all* of Kendell's friends were girls. So men, what do you think, when a man comes home and he sees his son hanging out with six girls, what goes through a man's mind? What are some of the questions that a man has? Having had this conversation with thousands of men I am going to share some of their thoughts with you. My expectation is that at least some of you are having the same thoughts right now that they did.

First thought that comes to many men's mind is "thumbs up" or "that's my boy." They admit that seeing their son with six girls makes them proud. For many men it shows that their son has sexual interest in girls and that girls like him, and that is a win-win situation.

Other men share that it might bring up concerns. When questioned about what concern it may bring up men admit that it may lead to questions about their son's sexual identity. The question is usually simply stated as, "Is he gay?" They would proceed to ask their son, "What are you doing with all those girls?" or questions like, "Which one do you like?" What men have told me is that as long as he likes one of the girls, all is well. I then ask well what if he doesn't like any of them and by chance he is not gay, what then? That question has the possibility of stumping men. They would ask their sons, "Which one do you like?" and their son would state, "I don't like any of them, Dad, they're just my friends."

And the father would say, "Well what do you do with them?" and the son would respond, "We just hang out, Dad, they're my friends."

Dad would say, "Yeah, I get that but what do you do? What do you talk about?"

The message that our sons and other boys are getting from far too many men, actually good men, is that outside of sexual

conquest boys should have limited interest in girls. The message
to our boys was and continues to be today that you can have a
girl or two as your friend, but more than that and your manhood
as we define it is in question. When it comes to the man box, I
believe that homophobia is the glue that keeps it together. We
teach our sons and other boys to define manhood by distancing
themselves from the experiences of women and girls; in order to
effectively distance oneself you have to also truly develop a lack
of interest. We then allow for limited interest, and that usually is
reserved for sexual conquest. While I am sure there are various
degrees of disagreement with me on this point, there is one reality to all of this that's difficult to challenge. You take the average
eighteen-year-old young man, good kid and all. You then take
the average eighteen-year-old young woman, and his interest in
her lessens when we take sexual conquest off the table. There are
no absolutes to anything I'm saying in this book and that relates
to this issue as well. I am not saying all eighteen-year-old boys;
I'm not saying your son. What I am saying is that, far too often,
this is the reality.

"If I control the purse strings, then I am in control of everything else too."

—James

Real Talk

Conversations with Everyday Men

This chapter is a select sampling of the thousands of conversations I have had with men individually or in small and large groups. In my work with my organization, A Call To Men, I have spent a lot of time studying the relationship between well-meaning men and the role we play in a society where men's violence against women is at epidemic proportions. I am passing on some of my shared experiences with men to help you reflect on your life as a well-meaning man. Far too often in our society women and girls are experiencing tragedy at the hands of boys and men because we have been taught that they are of less value than men and they are the property of men.

The discussions in this chapter are designed to help us recognize that as well-meaning men we have been taught knowingly and unknowingly to manage the fertile ground which allows abusive men to be who they are in the presence of good men. Well-meaning men far outnumber abusive men, but this chapter shows how we have some of the same perspectives. These conversations are aimed at helping well-meaning men see that in all of our goodness so much of our thinking and behaviors support a culture of male domination.

I believe in good men. When they are equipped with the reality and painstaking truth, our fathers, sons, brothers, and friends will step up to the plate and be accountable. I have included notes for you to reflect on some of those.

JAKE

As a man, I usually don't think about this kind of stuff. I never had actual conversations with men on manhood. Of course I recall on numerous occasions men in my life saying, men don't do this and men don't do that, but I don't recall many or any conversations on how to be a man. What goes on with a woman, whether she's having a problem with guys hitting on her or saying things to her, was not on my radar.

And when you talk about objectification of women this is all eye-opening to me. It never crossed my mind until right now that my way of looking at women had an effect on them. I admit that I objectify women on a daily basis without even really being conscious of it. I am beginning to really see things differently. It's funny how the bad guys get all the press, the ones who do the raping, slapping, and abusing. When in all actuality, the sexist attitude is coming from me too, from most men, the ones who are seen as the good guys.

I am beginning to accept the reality that my behavior as a man is important. Because I never broke the law or did anything illegal, I never associated my behaviors with that of abusive men. I do now realize that the small things that I do have a big impact on the day-to-day struggles of women.

TONY'S THOUGHTS

Jake is an example of how we as men are on what I call *remote control*—just doing things as we always have, and simply following tradition without question. This is very normal behavior for men. The exciting thing about Jake is that once his consciousness was raised about the issues of male domination, sexism, and violence against women, he began to rethink things. Jake began to be more of a critical thinker as it relates to manhood; in other words, he got *off remote control* and began to analyze his behavior and the behavior of other men. Jake is now positioned to challenge inappropriate behavior of men as well as teach sons and other boys healthy examples of manhood.

YOUR THOUGHTS

Are you on remote control?
Yes/No/Not Sure—Use the note space below to examine your thoughts.

_____

_____

_____

_____

_____

_____

Do you have conversations with men about manhood? Are those conversations for the purpose of promoting healthy

manhood? Do you share in conversations with boys about being healthy men?

_____

_____

_____

_____

_____

If promoting healthy manhood is your goal, what could you do more of?

_____

_____

_____

_____

_____

SHAKIR

How we objectify women is deep when I really allow myself to think about it. As a young man, I spend a lot of time watching music videos. I also have to agree that many of them are like soft porn and are getting more and more out of control. The messages in the music videos are if you are a man with money, you also have power, respect, and lots of beautiful women at your disposal to be used as you choose. The women are always close to being naked, gyrating, and dancing in a very sexual way around the men. The men also seem to ignore the women as if to say they are not impressed by the attention.

The message here is that if you're a man you can pick just one or have them all at the same time because you are in charge. A lot of times I actually see guys throwing money at the women in the videos, which say that women can be bought, further emphasizing the point that they are things, not human, play toys, and sexual objects. Ironically, my friends in the entertainment business tell me that most of the females in the videos are barely being paid, if at all.

What I have also found interesting is that we talk more about the women being inappropriate for dressing and dancing as they do. Rarely do we hold the men accountable for creating and sustaining the demand for this behavior. We don't talk enough about men as the benefactor of this behavior. Often we make it appear that this is solely a women's problem and we as men don't have anything to do with it.

TONY'S THOUGHTS

Shakir has developed great insight and understanding into the objectification of women in our society. He also makes the important connection between objectification and dehumanization. This connection is very important when seeking to understand violence against women. When we dehumanize a person or a people we are less sensitive to their experience. Unfortunately we as good men stand by and watch terrible things happen to women without considering an intervention. There are other factors that can contribute to our inaction, but the relationship between objectification and dehumanization is a big part of it.

YOUR THOUGHTS

Do you see the objectification of women as a major issue in our society?
Yes/No/Not Sure—Use the note space below to examine your thoughts.

_____

_____

_____

_____

_____

_____

What are some personal behaviors you can begin to challenge that support the objectification of women?

_____

_____

_____

_____

_____

What are some messages you would like to share with men and boys about this issue?

_____

_____

_____

_____

_____

_____

BILL

I'm an old guy, so in my day it was a lot easier when men were the protectors and providers for women. Men went to work, earned a living, stayed on a job for thirty years, got a gold watch and retired. We were expected to take care of the family and the wife would stay home and raise the kids. The wife was there when the kids got out of school; we didn't have to worry about kids being alone and all the issues that come with that today.

Parents taught their daughters that they should be able to cook, go to college, find a husband, get married, and raise a family. Nowadays, women are far more independent and want to work for whatever reason. They want to make the same amount of money as men. Women today seem to be okay with being single, some would actually rather have a relationship with another woman instead of a man.

Some women today (my sister for example) look down on men and feel like they don't need a man to take care of them.

My sister is always speaking about this, I think she just uses it as a justification as to why no man wants to marry her. Some men resent women for acting like we are not needed. I think this also makes many men feel intimidated. A successful woman says things like, "I don't need a man. I have my own money. I own a home. I have a nice car. I can get whatever I want." Things like this disrespect men. I believe women should understand these things about men and not purposefully try to deflate our pride. I hate to say it but I think women have brought this violence issue on themselves. Not that it's okay for anyone to be hit, I'm totally against that, but women have to acknowledge that they play a role in it.

TONY'S THOUGHTS

While Bill identifies himself as an old guy, and some of his views may seem to be outdated, there are many that share his views. Bill's views on women playing a role in the violence they experience at the hands of men are what we frequently hear from men, and women as well. The idea that women should understand the feelings of men and take the necessary action to ensure that our manhood is not damaged is also a frequent view I hear from men. This is an exercise in how dominating groups expect those who are experiencing marginalization to assist in maintaining it. This is also an example of when women choose to stand against marginalization or promote equality, they are, in turn, also viewed as responsible for the backlash against it.

Also, subtle in Bill's remarks but very important is the issue of women choosing to love women. Bill mentions it in a way that supports the notion that women who are lesbian, gay, queer, or transgender hate men. And, in fact, their views and positions on equality are not about ending the oppression of women but more about their hatred of men. This view just allows men to discredit these women's views and opinions, while enforcing heterosexism.

YOUR THOUGHTS

Do women play some role in the violence they experience at the hands of men?

Yes/No/Not Sure—Use the note space below to examine your thoughts.

_____

_____

_____

_____

_____

Would we be better off as a society if we revert back to more traditional gender roles?

_____

_____

_____

_____

_____

What are some things you are doing or can do to teach men and boys to promote equality? And to hold each other accountable for our behavior?

_____

_____

_____

_____

_____

_____

JOHN

I'm not gawking at females and I don't hit, smack, or even yell at women. But, I do know plenty of guys who do and I've never said a word to them. I understand now that my silence gives men who are abusive permission to do so. I never thought about it that way but it's true. I guess that makes me partly responsible too. I make it okay for them by minding my own business.

I must admit that just because I realize this is wrong doesn't mean I'm ready to do anything about it. I don't see myself saying anything to another man about his relationship with his girlfriend or wife. There are a few guys that are close to me, I could say something to them about the crude jokes they tell. I realize the camaraderie amongst guys gives me the power to stop it if I really wanted to. I could do better.

TONY'S THOUGHTS

John's increased knowledge on violence against women along with his understanding of the response or lack of response from good men is typical. When men are exposed to this information it is difficult to deny the truth of it. The challenge for men is to then take action. I don't discredit the progress that has been made by men like John in acknowledging the truths of manhood. However, simply acknowledging the truth won't move most men to action. I believe when staying silent to the truth becomes too uncomfortable, men will speak out.

YOUR THOUGHTS

What truths have you found in most of what you have read or learned about manhood and violence against women? Have those truths moved you to action?

Yes/No/Not Sure—If yes, please share. If no, please explain why not.

_____

_____

_____

_____

_____

What do you think the impact would be if we had a critical mass of men and boys speaking out?

_____

_____

_____

_____

_____

CARL

I am outraged by what we put up with in this society. As men we have to find a way to get involved. We also have to challenge the court system which appears hell bent on letting abusive men get away with it. We as men should be doing so much more to stop the violence.

Good men far outnumber men who are abusive. All of us should get together to outsmart abusive men; they think they can get away with the violence, expecting us to remain silent and mind our business. I must admit abusive men are pretty smart. They know what men will accept and how to push the envelope in a way that he doesn't get us up in arms.

They keep most of the verbal and physical abuse indoors. And if they slip up in front of us they keep it to just a slap or something like that. They abuse in the way that it might grab our attention but all we are going to do is watch and see if anything else is going to happen. I do not believe that abusers are sick people either. The sick ones probably would never be able to find a woman to marry him. They aren't sick, abusive men know exactly what they are doing. This abuser guy is cunning and cons some unsuspecting woman to commit to him. Then he smacks her around behind closed doors in privacy. He knows better than to do that in public. But, what that also means is that we allow him to do it in private. Many of us as good men know what he's doing in private. We simply treat it as none of our business. We have all been taught that saying, "What goes on in this house, stays in this house."

TONY'S THOUGHTS

Carl is sharing outrage that we don't often hear from men regarding violence against women. He has also developed a critical analysis of what's happening. Carl is not just spilling anger, he has a raised consciousness about the relationship between abusive men and nonabusive men. This is great insight and his outrage is acceptable.

YOUR THOUGHTS

Do you share in any of Carl's outrage about men's violence against women?
Yes/No/Not Sure—Use the note space below to examine your thoughts.

_____

_____

_____

_____

_____

How do you handle relationships with men who are abusive toward women? This includes inappropriate remarks and jokes. Do you usually challenge them, support them, or remain silent?

_____

_____

_____

_____

_____

_____

What's the overall message that we give as men by remaining silent to abusive language and behavior of men?

_____

_____

_____

_____

_____

_____

JAMES

Men are not going to willingly give up all of the power and let women be in charge. If I control the purse strings, then I am in control of everything else too. I control what you buy and when you buy it. Just the fact that if you want something you have to ask me is a form of control. You also have to be nice to me, do what I say, etc.

Financial control makes us feel powerful, which is why many men have a huge problem with dating or marrying a woman who makes more money than him. This is an interesting issue. Here you have a couple, at the end of the day if she makes more money that technically means *we* make more money. But for many men there is the need not only to earn more to call the shots, but also to feel like a man. The stuff in this man box really runs deep. It can really negatively impact a families' well-being. We live in a difficult time financially speaking, two incomes are needed just to make it, when you allow yourself to think about it, this mentality actually is ridiculous and oppressive.

In many respects I still don't think we have come that far as men, we still want women to stay in their place, emotionally and financially. For men to give all of that up would be a stretch. I know that men and women should be equal in a relationship since it's the right thing to do. I want to think that I am a fair guy. But, on this issue, I don't think I'm ready for true equality. I hate to admit that I like the power, but I do.

TONY'S THOUGHTS

I appreciate James's frankness on this issue of power. Not because I agree with him but it gives me the opportunity to address an area that many men continue to struggle with. You see, we no longer live in the society that Bill was referring to. Today we live in a dual-income society; not all but most households require dual incomes. I agree that many men are still challenged by women earning a higher income, and financial power is very much a part of the man box. Historically men make a connection to earned income and power. It should be noted that one of the ills still existing today in our male-dominating society is that women only earn seventy-eight cents to the dollar when doing the same exact job as men. This is an example of how our society values men as head of household, feeding this notion by giving us higher wages than women for the same work.

YOUR THOUGHTS

Do you believe men should have more power in a relationship?
Yes/No/Not Sure—Use the note space below to examine your thoughts.

_____

_____

_____

_____

_____

_____

What would shared power look like?

_____

_____

_____

_____

_____

_____

What are your thoughts about living in a society where women make less than men for doing the same exact job?

_____

_____

_____

_____

_____

KEN

I think that we live in a world where the expectations for men are very strong. If you fall short and grow up to be a man outside of the "man box," men *and women* will judge you (though I have seen change in this area with gay rights and all). Anyway, the truth be told, no woman wants a man who responds to things like "a woman." Also, no one wants to see a little boy responding to things like a little girl. Think about when you see a little boy prancing around or crying a lot. We automatically think, *something is wrong here.* I know I do. So, I jump in and say, "Hey, listen, men don't act this way. You need to be tough. You need to handle your business. Suck it up. Come on, be a man!" This sounds crazy actually. So I guess I would be wrong to come down that hard on a kid, but let's be *for real*, if we don't he's going to have a tough time growing up. Even if it's the right thing to do, what man is going to teach his son to be soft in this world, not too many.

TONY'S THOUGHTS

Ken's position is widely supported by both men and women. While men may believe the truths in the challenges we discussed regarding manhood, they don't want their sons to be the "pioneers" of the required change. I have found this to be true at times with women as well; whether it's their sons or the man they are partnered with, they are reluctant to let him go out of the man box completely. As Ken has mentioned, there is a great deal of progress being made. We have more young people today than ever before challenging and questioning traditional gender norms and sexual identities.

YOUR THOUGHTS

Are you flexible at all when teaching boys gender roles? Are you very traditional? Is it okay for boys to explore outside of the man box?

Yes/No/Not Sure—Use the note space below to examine your thoughts.

_____

_____

_____

_____

_____

_____

Do you make a connection between strict gender roles and violence against women?

_____

_____

_____

_____

_____

What are some of the ways we can support boys who choose not to adhere to the norms of the man box?

_____

_____

_____

_____

_____

VICTOR

My father had a considerable impact on my ideas around what it means to be a man. He taught me a lot about the man box.

Growing up, I never heard him say I love you, even though he would tell me he was proud of me and stuff like that. I never saw him cry though we had a lot bad experiences in our family. I grew up in a tough neighborhood so I assume that had a lot to do with his thinking. He wasn't tough on my sister, but I don't recall him telling her or my mother that he loved them.

I remember being thirteen and my father would constantly get on my case for being so emotional. For some reason, it was a crazy time for me and I was sensitive to the slightest thing. Even I thought something must be wrong with me, crying like a girl at the drop of a hat. He used to say, "I'm tired of you crying all the time. Are you on drugs?" He knew I wasn't using drugs. I found his questioning to me to be quite interesting because he equated being emotional to the erratic behavior of an addict. He was letting me know clearly that being emotional meant something was wrong with me. My father had some strong feelings about me being emotional.

I believe that I might have been depressed back then as a boy. There was a lot going on in my life that I could not handle. Instead of my father being loving, kind, and gentle with me, he was tough. Instead of him showing genuine concern for me, he was mean. Never once did he or my mother think about getting me some help, someone to talk with. I don't think my father wanted to offer help at all; he just wanted me to get myself together, under control.

He would say things like, "Let your little sister cry. That's for her. But, you're not supposed to be crying all the time. You are a boy, not a girl." My father's message was consistent and left a great impact on me. He made it clear that I was to keep my emotions in check because I was supposed to be stronger than a woman. In his eyes, crying was a sign of weakness. I wanted to make my father proud of me, so I followed what he told me. If I was hurting, I would suck it up. I learned to perform this way well over the years, in many cases, to my own demise. If I didn't, I am afraid to think of the kind of relationship I would have had with my father. I was and remain today, even though he has been dead a long time, loyal to my father.

TONY'S THOUGHTS

Victor's story speaks to father and son relationships on many levels. Fathers believe in what manhood consists of and take it as their responsibility to teach those principles to their sons. Fathers pass this knowledge on, in many cases, without question. Sons desire to be loyal to their fathers even when it goes against their own will. Like most men, this was Victor's experience.

YOUR THOUGHTS

Do you identify with any of the experiences of Victor, either with your dad or your son?
Yes/No/Not Sure—Use the note space below to examine your thoughts.

_____

_____

_____

_____

_____

What are your thoughts, pros and cons, on boys expressing their emotions or stuffing them away?

_____

_____

_____

_____

_____

Victor spoke about possibly being depressed. What are your thoughts about men and hidden depression?

_____

_____

_____

_____

_____

BOB

I am struggling with how to pass on some of this information to men I know and spend time with. I'm thinking about my fishing buddies, and then there are the guys I play poker with, or my friends at the classic car shows. I will admit it would be hard to go and start this conversation with them. I know that most men do not want to deal with discussing manhood. I don't know many men who would sit through that conversation, let alone participate, but we all should.

I definitely want to share this with men, although I don't know how to do so without making them uncomfortable or coming off preachy. I will have to find a way because I think this issue is very important. Right now, I am already thinking of what I need to do to change, how I can respond differently to my wife and the other women around me. I can stand to make some adjustments in my own life.

TONY'S THOUGHTS

Bob's dilemma is that of many men; it's not easy to develop a voice to talk about male domination, manhood, and violence against women. We are in the midst of the first generation of men choosing to speak out as a critical mass. This is new for men with no foundation to rest upon. There are many risk factors that men speak of: Am I going to lose my friends? Will men think differently about me? What am I going to have to give up? While these are fair questions, I ask men to rather focus on: What will be the benefit to women? What are the benefits to society? What do I have to gain?

YOUR THOUGHTS

Developing a voice to talk about these issues takes practice. Are you open to it? How do you plan to hone this skill?
Yes/No/Not Sure—Use the note space below to examine your thoughts.

Can you see how not developing a voice supports men who are abusive? Is it okay for men to remain silent?

What do you think the impact will be on our sons and other boys if we as men normalized speaking about issues of male domination and the man box?

CURTIS

My wife is into exercise and goes out early in the morning to walk or jog. Every morning she is up at 5 a.m., dressed, and out the door. Recently she asked me to get her some pepper spray and I could not understand why because we live in a nice, suburban neighborhood. I was shocked when she asked me. Naturally, I assumed that she was safe. I thought she was being paranoid, thinking to myself who's going to mess with her around here.

I realized that my wife can't tell the good guys from the bad guys because all men are looking at her the same way. That being said, women have to think about their safety a lot more than I ever imagined. I never realized that she could feel unsafe around regular guys. If she is alone and notices someone checking her out, she doesn't know what's next. She doesn't know if it's going to escalate from "hey baby" to "hey bitch."

So my wife has to have her guard up while she tries to figure out if someone is just looking or if they are contemplating approaching her. As I sit here, I am now wondering if a woman has ever felt unsafe around me based on the way I was looking at her.

TONY'S THOUGHTS

I have had numerous conversations with women over the years regarding their experiences loving men, sharing community with men, and being afraid for their safety all at the same time.

I appreciate Curtis's enlightenment; far too many men have no idea of women's experiences in society and what it's like for them sharing community with men. Where to park their car, leaving after dark in numbers, not getting on elevators by themselves, but not taking the stairs either, etc., etc., etc. I think as men begin to truly appreciate the experiences of women we will become more supportive, responsible, and accountable.

YOUR THOUGHTS

Have you ever had a purposeful conversation with women in your life about their experiences with men in their community? Yes/No/Not Sure—Use the note space below to examine your thoughts.

_____

_____

_____

_____

_____

_____

How often do you think women in your life think about their safety on a given day?

_____

_____

_____

_____

_____

Other than protecting women, what can we as men do to challenge this reality?

_____

_____

_____

_____

_____

_____

As a man, you only have permission to turn down sex when you have been married or partnered for a while.

Our Relationships with Women
A Selection of My Favorite Man Box Stories

Welcome to a selection of my favorite man box stories. While some of the stories are entertaining, what's most important is that they make us as men reflect on our individual experiences with women in our community, particularly our wives, girlfriends, mothers, bosses, neighbors, and others. I will admit at times it's healthy to make fun of ourselves as men in dealing with women. However, it is important to keep in mind that we should never laugh at the expense of women and the negative experiences they have had at the hands of men. At the end of the day, these stories are intended to teach; hence, we can learn to become better men. When I was putting this book together I felt it important that it should not reflect my experiences alone; the issues in manhood are universal and real, and whether we as men want to admit it or not, we have work to do to heal our past, present, and future relationships with women. I believe we can do it.

JIM

Jim is a sixty-year-old friend of mine. This story happened over thirty-five years ago while he was attending college.

Jim and his college friend (who has since become a lifelong friend) were hanging out at a bar. They met two women and the four of them spent the evening together having drinks and talking. When it was time to leave, the women invited the guys to their apartment. As soon as they got there, Jim's friend and one of the women headed straight for the bedroom, which left Jim and the other woman alone. It was clear the woman with Jim was attracted to him and wanted to take him to her bedroom, if he was interested. Jim told me that though he found the woman to be very nice and attractive, he was not interested in having sex with her. As time went on Jim found himself becoming increasingly uncomfortable, trying to make small talk to pass the time.

After about twenty minutes of discussing current events, the weather, and what college courses he liked and didn't like, Jim decided it was time to leave. He said goodnight to the woman and knocked on the bedroom door to tell his friend that he was leaving. Since Jim was driving, as expected, his friend was quite irritated because that would mean he would have to cut his activities short.

Some thirty-five years later, whenever Jim is with his old friend, he is reminded of that day. Jim explains that, let's say, they are out to dinner and their wives leave to go to the restroom. An attractive woman passes by their table, and *bam*, his friend will bring it up. "Remember back in college when you decided you didn't want to have sex and you made me leave?"

LET'S SUMMARIZE THIS

Jim's story is a good illustration of the man box at work. The fact that Jim did not want to have sex was not only inconceivable to his friend but also unforgettable. Men are socialized to never turn down sex. In many cases they are taught that sexual conquest is the primary goal of most relationships with women. Refusal to take advantage of an opportunity to have sex, according to the man box, means something is wrong with you as a man. In fact, other men will start to question or challenge your manhood. As a man, you only have permission to turn down sex when you have been married or partnered for a while. Under those circumstances, you can be tired and just not feel like it. In Jim's situation, peer pressure did not get the best of him, but the fact that there is pressure for men and boys to have sex is a problem. It is admirable for a woman to be a virgin, whereas it can be shameful for men and boys. Here, the man box pressures males in cases where they may not be ready to have sex or the woman is not interested. This man box thinking lays the groundwork for violent situations such as rape and other forms of sexual assault. When you have men trying to prove themselves by engaging in sex, violence may not be far away.

PAUL

I can remember, starting around the age of five, my father leaving home going on business trips. My oldest sister Sharon at the time was ten. My father as he was preparing to leave would look at me and say, "Paul, Dad is leaving on a business trip, you're the man of the house, take care of your mother, sisters, and little brother." I would say, "Yes, Dad" and stick my little chest out, my mother would just smile and my sister Wanda would roll her eyes at me. Later that evening around eight o'clock I would go to bed. Like most nights I would lay there and try to go to sleep, but after an hour or so I couldn't take it a minute longer. You see, there was a monster peeping at me from the closet the whole time.

So out of the bed I would go, with my feet barely hitting the floor I would run down the hall to my sister Sharon's room. She would be sitting on a chair in her room reading a book or playing music. I would begin to beg, asking to let me sleep with her. She would hold out for a few minutes just to make me beg more and sweat some, then saying with a look of disgust on her face "get in the bed." Relieved, I would jump up in her bed and get under the covers for safety. As I was pulling the covers up to my neck I would look at her and say, "But don't forget, I'm in charge"; she would just look at me and laugh.

LET'S SUMMARIZE THIS

When men tell their sons they are the man of the house at the age of five to ten it's actually preparation for the future. You see, men know that when their son is five he's not in charge of anything. Like me, I was going to bed at eight o'clock, what was I in charge of? The truth of the matter is I was in charge of nothing. So when men tell their sons they are the man of the house and in charge, what actually is happening is preparation for the future. Well, what future? For men the future is when our sons have their own families, we are ensuring they will be ready to be in charge. Think about it, we rarely tell our daughters they are in charge, unless they're the oldest and both parents are going to be away from the home.

A fair thing to ask men to do is examine the subtle messages when we tell our sons they're in charge. For example, what are we saying about his mother when we tell him he is in charge? The subtle messages rooted in male socialization are: She is not in charge, she is incapable of being in charge, she needs a man to take charge, she needs a man to take care of her, she can't be trusted, etc. In addition, there are messages that a daughter experiencing her brother being placed in charge receives as well. For example, your brother is worthy of being in charge regardless of his limitations and you are not, you need a man to take care of you, you are not and never will be as good as a boy. Now we as men don't intentionally mean for any of this to be the case or outcome. We are just trying to raise our sons to be good men. The challenge is that we are on remote control, doing things the way they have always been done. It's required for men to get off remote control and think through these issues as we focus on the next generation of men.

JOHN

John was about twenty-five years old at the time of this story; we had worked together for many years.

John enrolled in karate school and began taking lessons for beginners. In his class there was a woman that he found attractive, so eventually he asked her out on a date. They soon became good friends, enjoying karate classes together and also dating on a regular basis.

Everything was going well and the relationship continued to grow. After a while, John decided he didn't want to take karate lessons and stopped going, but his new girlfriend continued. Within a few years, she became a karate expert. Even though everything was going well in their relationship, John stated that he was becoming more and more uncomfortable with the fact that his girlfriend was a karate expert.

When John allowed himself to look deeper at his insecurity, it had *everything* to do with her being a karate expert. His real concern was that she could actually "whip his butt" if she wanted. He admitted that his anxiety was sort of childish and immature, but he could not shake that awkward feeling. John talked about how embarrassed he was around his friends when conversations came up about their wives and girlfriends. John said he would try to downplay her karate skills around his guy friends, but it didn't work. They would tease him about having a girlfriend who could "whip his butt" and keep him in his place.

John ultimately ended the relationship. Now, he feels bad for succumbing to the pressure he felt from his friends. John was so affected by his friends giving him a hard time about being weaker than his girlfriend he wanted to get out of the relationship. This sounds like a situation between kids, but this happened in John's adult years.

LET'S SUMMARIZE THIS

John's situation is a common issue among well-meaning men. The difference is most men would not have ventured into a relationship where they felt the woman was physically stronger than them or, in John's case, a karate expert. Men find it hard to be with a woman who is taller, bigger, stronger, more powerful, or who even makes more money than them. The aforementioned characteristics (rooted in the socialization of manhood) have a tendency to make men feel that they are less powerful, which can make them feel like less of a man. This manifestation of the man box leads many men to believe that they absolutely have to be dominating, powerful, and in control with regard to women; anything less would be unmanly.

TED

Ted Bunch, cofounder of A Call To Men, describes an experience with a church.

In Ted's story, it appears that a long-standing member of a church had assaulted his wife. This member was in a leadership role within the church and had many family members in the congregation. The woman had been badly assaulted, which meant that there had to be some type of intervention and "sweeping it under the carpet" was not an option. Someone suggested to the pastor that they put together a domestic violence policy for the ministry leadership. That same person knew of Ted's work and set up a meeting with him and the pastor.

The pastor met with Ted and provided all the details of the situation. Ted listened to him and noticed that he was visibly stressed about how to handle the situation because the accused was a known leader in the church. The pastor appeared to have a dilemma; he knew that a response was required but he was concerned about the impact it might have on a large portion of his congregation that were family members of the abuser. At some point in the conversation, Ted asked the pastor, "What would you do if he had hit you?"

The pastor quickly replied, "Oh, he would have to leave this church. I would encourage him to remain within the body of Christ, but he would have to worship somewhere else."

Then, Ted simply stated, "So there's your policy."

LET'S SUMMARIZE THIS

While the solution seemed simple, it was really circumstantial for the pastor. If the man had hit him, he would clearly consider it to be an assault, an attack, and a crime. However, because the man hit a woman (his wife), a host of other questions and concerns came into play. What was her part in the situation? Did she provoke him? Should the church be addressing this private matter? Is it any of my business what goes on between a man and his wife? What impact will my decision have on the church? The pastor, a well-meaning, religious man, was operating under the pretense that the woman assaulted "belonged" to the man, and that the crime may be none of his business. Again, we see the collective socialization of manhood influencing how well-meaning men deal with and process violence against women.

DAVE

Dave's story was told to me by one of his friends who were present. It's a classic inner city man box story.

Dave's story involves him and five of his friends standing on a street corner. An attractive woman passes by and they all look her up and down. Only one guy, we'll call him Mr. Gift of Gab—you know, the one who always has something to say—proceeds to say, "Baby you're so fine I could . . ." Most of the time, women would just ignore the inappropriate comments made by Mr. Gift of Gab as if they were used to it, but this day was different. The woman turned around and let him have it.

She quickly told him off without cursing or yelling. After Dave and his friends witnessed her verbal tongue lashing, they let out a harmonious, "Oooohhhh!" I asked Dave to explain what that response meant. He said that the guys were basically teasing Mr. Gift of Gab because he had been humiliated by a woman, which is worse than being humiliated by a man. He let a woman disrespect him in front of his boys and the man box says that is unacceptable. Feeling that his manhood was at stake, Mr. Gift of Gab retaliated, going back and forth with this woman, insistent on having the last word. It became obvious that he was no match for her, but he just could not let it go. What would his friends think of him if he did? They were already laughing uncontrollably. That was their way of saying we see you losing to a female and we are not going to let you forget it. This woman was undoubtedly knocking this guy right out of the man box. Eventually, Mr. Gift of Gab got desperate, became angry, and started cursing and threatening to assault the woman. He also attempted to go after her. Dave said he and the guys had to physically restrain him, as he continued to intimidate and verbally dehumanize her. Once Mr. Gift of Gab saw that she was retreating, he felt like a man again and back in good standing with the guys by the standards of the man box since he had overpowered her. He could face the guys now because he had proven that he was better than her, even if he had to do so through violent and aggressive behavior.

LET'S SUMMARIZE THIS

This situation demonstrates that when a man is placed among other men, he will do whatever he can to maintain his man status, especially when a woman challenges him in front of this group. Keep in mind, for the most part, this was a group of well-meaning men. Nevertheless, male status and domination over women are everyday practices.

GARY

My wife and I owned an old Victorian house. We decided that we wanted to renovate the kitchen. We began by gutting it down to the studs and starting from there. I have always been pretty good with my hands when it comes to building things. The renovations included sheet-rocking, painting, and general handyman work. No problem. I never studied or took any courses in woodworking or construction. I didn't need to; I just used common sense and my manly intuition.

I remember when my daughter Sharon bought me a tool belt for Christmas. That tool belt transformed me into a proud poster boy for the man box every time I put it on. I felt like I was one with masculinity.

I definitely know how to pound a nail into a piece of wood. But my wife, on the other hand, actually did know what type of nail should be used. She just happened to be a student of many things. But, I was the one who took the lead on the project without asking a lot of input from her. I would go about my business tearing stuff down and putting other things up.

Whenever my wife entered the kitchen, I could feel my "man stuff" in me thinking, *Why are you in here? What do you want? Can't you see that I'm working?* And please! Don't let her ask any questions about my work or stand in the middle of the floor looking around. If she did happen to start questioning me, I could feel my "man stuff" rise up from my toes and start blowing out of my ears. It doesn't feel good to admit this, but when she was examining my work, I would get very edgy.

For this reason, my wife would rarely share her thoughts or opinions about the project. Of course, my male friends could stop by while I was working and give me their two-cents and I would welcome their opinions. Ironically, my wife is smarter and more knowledgeable than most of my friends. After reflecting back on that project, I could see that I considered my wife's input to be less valuable than my friends. I also realized that if she was giving me instructions on something that has been defined as "man's work," I felt like less of a man—per the teachings of the man box. I would actually feel like I was outside of the box.

LET'S SUMMARIZE THIS

In further conversation with Gary, he stated, "The challenge for me and other men as well is to value women equally and redefine what has been ingrained in us about women for so long. We should genuinely value their opinions, thoughts, suggestions, recommendations, or directives involved with any issue. Once we set these thoughts into motion and value women as we would men, we can retract the (man stuff) sexism that makes us think that we are worth more and that they are worth less. I'm not sure that men actually feel "less than" in these kinds of situations or that many of us can even name what we are feeling. I just know that we often resort to feeling annoyed, agitated, and, of course, angry because that's what the man box teaches us is okay."

MARK

This is one of my favorite man box stories. It took place at Mark's neighborhood home improvement store, where the man box is alive and well.

A few years ago, my wife and I were remodeling a bathroom in our home. She wanted me to panel the walls, not a full sheet of panel, but more like a half panel. So, off we go to the home improvement store. Now, based on the rules of the man box, as we enter the store, without the need to discuss it, it should already be known . . . that I'm to do all the talking—this is man box stuff.

We walked around the store for about ten minutes looking for the half panel before I decided to ask for some help. As with most things, I'd rather handle them myself without asking for help, but I looked everywhere and could not find that half panel. Once we approached one of the male salespersons, my wife stood there quietly as I started talking.

The conversation between me and the male salesperson unfolds like this:

"Hey, how you doing?" I ask.

"Good and yourself?" he responds.

"Great, thanks. I'm looking for a half panel. You know, the half sheet of panel that you can put a nice piece of molding around."

"I'm not sure what you mean, sir."

"Come on, the half sheet of panel, man? You know what I'm talking about."

This went back and forth for about a minute or so until my wife, tired of watching me make a fool out of myself, decides to get involved. "Wainscoting," she says.

This male salesperson, obviously not up on the rules of the man box, then made a serious violation. Based on the rules of the man box in that situation he was supposed to maintain eye contact with me and pretend like my wife never said a word. Instead, this man breaks the code and rejects collusion. He looks right at my wife and says, "Oh, wainscoting! Of course we have plenty."

"Great, do you have many styles?" she asks.

At this point, the two of them are having a conversation and have conveniently left me out of it. He then says to her "right this way," and they start walking toward the wainscoting and I follow feeling like a third wheel. They may as well have locked arms, held hands or something because that's the way it felt to me. My man box card had been rejected.

LET'S SUMMARIZE THIS

This story speaks to how men can step outside the man box and challenge its teachings. The truth of the matter is if we want to have true equality in our country, it's required for men to step out of the man box. Supporting women of course is one example; equally if not more important is what we are teaching our sons and other boys. We will discuss just that in the next chapter.

The man box produces a desire in men to not be vulnerable. Being vulnerable means not being in control.

Young Men of Character
Tackling Sports Culture and Manhood

Through my work with athletics I spend a great deal of time with coaches. I have come to understand the role they play in the lives of men and boys. Coaches are one of those groups of men that other men look up to. This means coaches have a tremendous influence on the thinking of men. This chapter speaks to that influence and the responsibility of coaches. At the same time we are also talking about mentors, teachers, fathers, youth workers, and any man that's spending time with our sons and other boys. As you read this chapter, please think beyond coaches (unless you are one), look for yourself.

Our boys and young men are faced with many challenges today regarding how we define what it means to be a man. While there are wonderful things about being a man, far too many of the characteristics hold our boys hostage, while negatively impacting their ability to develop into healthy and respectful men. Far too many definitions of manhood tell our boys to deny feelings of pain and hurt, and that anger is the only emotion they have permission to express. Our boys are challenged to not be soft or too nice, too friendly, too gentle, too kind or loving—don't be a punk or a sucker.

We should ask ourselves how we would want to see boys and young men behave in the world we want for the girls we love. Whatever that positive behavior is that we would want to see from boys and young men, it will *not* happen just by chance. The behavior that we would want to see from boys and young men as it relates to our daughters and other girls requires men to be part of their development.

I remember asking a twelve-year-old football player how he would feel if his coach told him in front of all the other players that he was playing like a girl. When asking the question I thought the boy would say, "I would be mad or sad." But to my surprise, he went as far as to say, "It would destroy me." As a coach it's important to think about the ways in which one motivates boys to perform at their best. Every time a coach tells a boy that he's playing like a girl, the follow-up thought should be, *what are we as coaches then saying about girls?*

The characteristics of what it means to be a man aid in creating what I call the Cycle of Consequences from Boys to Men. We have these rigid definitions of manhood creating negative experiences for many of our boys and young men. The socialization of manhood, with all its goodness also teaches some rigid definitions of what it means to be a man: Be tough, strong, athletic, aggressive, no fear, no pain, and always in control. While there is not necessarily anything wrong with being tough and strong— for example, I love football, I love watching tough, strong men play the game of football. The question is what if I'm not tough, what if I'm not strong, what if I'm very loving and gentle? What if I want to be loving, kind, and gentle while being tough and strong at the same time? What if I want to speak about my pain, hurts, and fears? There is a reason why our boys and young men work so very hard to fit into these rigid definitions of manhood, even if it's not who they are. Is this what we truly want for our boys? Is it working well? Does it contribute to many of our social problems? I believe these are fair questions to ask those of us who are men.

The man box produces a desire in men to not be vulnerable. Being vulnerable means not being in control. Being vulnerable means not taking risks and, most importantly, it includes not showing or even owning our feelings as men. If boys and men can't express feelings and if asking for help is a sign of weakness, it often results in lack of achievement, low self-worth, and stagnation. These results also produce excessive trauma for many boys and men as well as inappropriate behavior. The unfortunate thing, within all of this, is that our boys and young men then rely on what got them in the challenging situations to begin with, which is the man box. So the cycle begins for many boys and young men. A cycle of consequences, that without help, far too many of them can't get off.

I just made reference to our sons and boys needing help. What's both interesting and challenging about this is that a part of male socialization is to not ask for help. We have been taught as men that asking for help is a sign of weakness. When you think about it, it sounds weird. Why would asking for help be viewed as a sign of weakness? It comes back to the need for men to be in control and not be vulnerable; asking for help is a violation of both. So we grow up as men needing help, but not being allowed to ask for it. We are also taught that to offer help to a man is a violation as well.

I believe that coaches, fathers, mentors, and men in general have the opportunity to prevent or interrupt this cycle of consequences our boys and young men experience. I believe that we as men have a responsibility to assist boys and young men in their journey to manhood. I also believe and know that our boys not only need assistance from men, they also respond well to it.

Over the years I have witnessed and participated in numerous events where athletes spoke of the importance and the difference we as men can make in the lives of boys and young men. Many of the men shared personal experiences with coaches and other men and the impact they had on their lives. Men who witness these conversations by and large are moved by the experiences shared. During one event, an athletic director for a major university made a profound statement that will have a lasting impact on me. He stated, "While I had great respect for my teachers growing up as a young man, I can't remember their names, but I can remember the name of every athletic coach I ever played for." He shared his statement to emphasize the point that coaches have a lifelong effect on boys and young men. My son is a high school football player and his coach is a household name among our family. My wife and I are fortunate that his coach is a wonderful man and teaches the boys about healthy manhood, and uses football as a tool for character development. I am certain my son (along with many other boys) will maintain a lifelong relationship with this man.

As men we have a responsibility to be interrupters and pre-venters of this cycle of consequences in the lives of boys and young men. It's our responsibility to steer them in the right direction. As men we have a responsibility to create an environment where boys and young men feel comfortable sharing their feelings, expressing their fears, and, most importantly, asking for help. Such an environment will also require men to model what they teach, allowing themselves to be vulnerable, sharing openly, and demonstrating love and compassion.

Envision a football coach at the end of a practice sur-rounded by forty boys all on one knee looking up at him. At that time he has their undivided attention. At that moment he's more important than their mother, father, and possibly anyone else in the world. It leads me to think, at that moment what a wonderful time to talk with them about something other than football. What a wonderful time to have a conversation with our boys and young men about being men of integrity, substance, and character.

Another area of importance when working with coaches and those involved in athletic sports is having purposeful con-versations about sports culture. I have worked for many years with high school, collegiate, and professional athletes. It's with-out question that sports culture can have a major impact on pro-moting healthy manhood.

When defining sports culture we can come up with many conflicting messages and teachings. For example, sports culture teaches aggression, domination, power, no fear, no pain, etc. But it also teaches teamwork, commitment, loyalty, dedication, and integrity. Sports culture has been known to teach *win at all costs*.

The challenge that's ahead of us is how to hold on to the wonderful aspects of sports culture that teach teamwork and commitment, and let go of the aspects of it promoting less value in women and heterosexism.

We can begin by having critical conversations of how manhood is far too often taught to men and boys through a lens that requires distancing oneself from the perceived experiences of women and girls.

Although outside of sports culture, one example occurred when my organization, A Call To Men, was asked to be part of a response to a tragic rape that had occurred on a college campus. A young woman was raped by a male student at the college. When we arrived at the school there was a large community meeting in process. Not only was this a horrifying event on the campus, but the young woman happened to be one of the most popular students attending the school. She was a star athlete, a leader in student government, and a very well-liked person. Because of the horrific crime and the victim's stature in the campus life, this was truly a galvanizing event for the college community. The meeting was held in the largest venue that the college had to offer and there was standing room only.

The main topic was how the college could make the campus safer for women immediately and in the long term. The discussion led to creating phone trees, buddy systems for the female students, and securing additional transports of cars and vans to shuttle the female students from point A to point B, particularly during the evening hours.

This approach lowers the risk of young women being assaulted and helps them feel safe. While it appears that this is an

appropriate response, what we are neglecting is that we are holding women responsible for doing something about violence being
perpetrated by men. Not only are we holding women responsible,
we are also inconveniencing them in the name of safety, while
men's lives go uninterrupted; this is a normal pattern of response
to violence against women in our communities. A Call To Men
was asked to participate because men need to be part of the solution, so we went to work. We asked the following questions:

"Was the person who raped the woman a male or female?"
The answer was a male.

"What if instead of transporting the young women from the
cafeteria to the dorm, the dorm to the library . . . we transported
the young men? If a man is the culprit why are we inconveniencing women for the violence that men perpetrate?"

Women in the room let out a loud roar in agreement.

The reaction by the women was not what we were going for
but it confirmed that this type of response was long overdue. It
was a revolutionary idea to say the least and we got a lot of push
back from some of the male administrators. One man even said
that we would be "gender profiling" if we transported men. We
reminded him that we could use his argument for sexual assault
on college campuses, that *is* gender profiling. Or that requiring
all the women on campus to utilize this bus and van service was
"gender profiling."

Our approach was a way to make the rape on that campus
the men's issue that it needed to be. The focus becomes on the
men. So the male students who are transported in the car or the
van are no longer asking about what the victim was wearing, or
why she was wherever she was, or nitpicking what she was doing

when she was raped. They are asking, "Who did this?" And saying, "We need to do something about it because I am not going
to be transported around campus for the rest of the year."

When we think about domestic violence and sexual assault
we tend to give the benefit of the doubt to the man—our default
setting is to lean on the side of men. Frankly, in our sexist and
patriarchal society, women are often inconvenienced and even
held accountable for the things that men do to them.

In the end, the school did transport the male students
instead of the young women for one month while they improved
their policy in response to sexual assault. They did not make the
decision because it was the right thing to do, but because of cost
associated with the transportation. It was a bottom line decision.
On campus there were less male students than female. The campus was about 40 percent male and it would take significantly
less resources. Fewer men to transport meant less money, less
staff time, fewer vehicles, etc. We were not so concerned about
how the decision was made but more that it changed the way
that sexual assault was looked at on that campus and it became
a men's issue.

A lack of interest in the experiences of women and girls
starts at an early age, as discussed in chapter two. Let's revisit
this again in a little more detail. From birth to about age five,
we (meaning, a male-dominating society) have a tendency to
allow little boys to share equally in the same experiences as little
girls. From about age five to ten we began to instill in boys the
importance of distancing themselves from girls to define their
manhood. What we see at this time is boys displaying a dislike
for girls (lack of interest), wanting to have little to do with them,

outside of teasing, often as a means to acknowledge their growing distaste.

Around the age of sixteen boys become physically attracted
to girls. Keep in mind that since the age of five they have been
taught to have a lack of interest. So we (again, a male-dominating society), at this time, make an exception for our boys: They
are allowed to have interest in the experience of girls related
to sexual/physical attraction. Granted, I'm not a sociologist or
psychologist, but the truth of the matter is the average eighteen-
year-old heterosexual young man has limited interest in the
average eighteen-year-old heterosexual young women outside of
sexual conquest. There are no absolutes, and again, we are not
talking about an exact science, but we are discussing reality. The
truth of the matter is you take an average eighteen-year-old heterosexual young man, and his interest in the average eighteen-
year-old heterosexual young woman doesn't extend too far past
sexual conquest. He's a good kid, I'm not taking a position at
all about his character or integrity; nevertheless, based on his
socialization from birth to eighteen, if you take sexual conquest
off the table his interest in females plummets. Now that's not to
say that eighteen-year-old young women are not interested in
sexual relationships. What I am saying is that they are not socialized having their primary interest to be sexual conquest.

I know I'm leaning hard into this whole issue of lack of
interest in women and girls, but I believe it's extremely important when viewing aspects of sports culture. We, unfortunately,
have a history of heterosexism that has denounced and devalued
girls and the LGBTQ and nongender conforming communities.
As a result of these norms in sports culture, we find ourselves

holding boys hostage to hyper notions of masculinity when it's not who they are or, in many cases, want to be, but feel society is demanding it of them.

A society that teaches a lack of interest in women and girls also limits a holistic experience of development for boys to men. A society that teaches a lack of interest in women and girls contributes to the foundation of men's violence against women. We know that today men's violence against women is in epidemic proportions—it's one of the leading causes of injury to women in our country.

Sports is one of the major influencers of male socialization and paramount in the development of boys to men. This is regardless of whether they play sports or not. Think of the time spent between youth sports and professional sports, for most men it's a lifetime of daily participation on one level or another.

Sports culture and those who influence it have the opportunity to better promote equality, to engage in our healing for a collective liberation for us all.

ESTABLISH THE CONNECTION

I have seen this clearly in my work with the National Football League. I have been a life skills trainer with the NFL for the past twelve years. I can remember when I first started; I knew I was going to be in a room with fifty-three professional football players. I was trying to figure out what I was going to say to them that would really grab their attention. I only had an hour with them. These are men who always have someone talking to them about something, mandatory training for this or that. The training sessions are scheduled right at the end of football practice so I'm the obstacle between the field and going home after a long day of working out in the heat or cold.

Some players would be having a winning season. Some players would be having a losing season. If they are having a winning season, they want to go ahead and enjoy that they are winning, get on with their day. They don't want to sit and talk to me. If they are having a losing season, they want to figure out how to win. They don't want to sit and talk to me. I was bringing a training session to them that was mandatory, which, by definition, was not exciting to them. So as the coach came in and introduced me and told them they had better pay attention, I was not feeling too confident that these guys really wanted to hear from me. I was a little nervous in front of these extremely powerful—physical and otherwise—men. So I began my session with a series of questions: What is the world you want to see for your daughters? How do you want to see men acting in that world? What kind of man do you want your son to be? And how will he become that man?

The average NFL player is about twenty-five years old, and some in the room had children already. Even the players who were a bit older that have children, none on average would be over twelve years old. An NFL career as a player is short. It takes three years to make it, by five years you're considered a veteran, and, for most, their career is over by eight years. On a team roster of fifty-three active players on average, there will be no more than five with double-digit years. So my audience was mostly young fathers with young children. As of today, I have facilitated this training session numerous times with different groups of players, and every time I started out with that same set of questions, I immediately got their attention. They were quickly in my hands because what was being discussed in the room became important to them. I had their attention. I had their interest. I had reached in and grabbed their hearts. They cared about the world their daughters live in.

Making this kind of connection is crucial, especially with men who dominate our sports culture. As a man who has worked with high school, collegiate, and professional sports organizations for many years, I am convinced that sports culture can have a major impact on promoting healthy manhood because it may be the single-handed most influential institution in our society for males.

We can begin by having critical conversations of how manhood requires distancing oneself from the perceived experiences of women and girls. When men envision the world that they want to see for their daughters to live in and how they want to see men acting and behaving in that world, not only do we gain interest in this conversation, but it also puts men in conflict against themselves. They know what they are. They know what they're male friends are. They also know that they can't spend all their waking hours making sure that no man mistreats their daughters. Through their daughters, these men take harder looks at themselves. And then the light bulbs come on.

We do realize that we have contributed to the problem. We do realize that it may change or may not change in the time that our daughters come of age. We do realize that doing nothing will lead to nothing.

FIRST STEP—MOVE TO ACTION . . . OR NOT

Those of us who do the work of engaging men in healthy, respectful conversations about manhood realize that the trainings and conversations don't immediately move all men to action. In some cases, it does move men. Some men look at how they are going to work differently with their sons and other boys. Some men think differently about their wives and other women in their lives and begin moving closer toward equality in those relationships. As you read in the previous chapter, some men will say, "This is good information, but I don't think I am ready to put it into practice because of the challenges it would present for me."

Once men digest the information, they find themselves in all different places. At A Call To Men, we have experienced very little resistance in men acknowledging that this is a truth.

From this point, we have seen men move forward in the moment. And we have seen men move forward later on. We know that there are men who move forward, as well as men who make the choice not to. It's a process for most men; we didn't get where we are overnight.

I have come to learn that men are listening. I'm both encouraged and full of hope. This is not to say we don't still have a lot of work because we do, but I'm encouraged. I was in the gym recently with my son. I was on the treadmill, which was on one side of the gym. He was lifting free weights on another side of the gym. I saw a guy talking to him while he was lifting the free weights. My son was doing squats, and he was talking to him about the correct position of his back and stuff like that. I was peeking over and saw the man leave. At that point, my son came over and told me the guy was asking about me. "He asked if you were my dad and I said yes. He then said he thought he knew you from someplace and asked if you did public speaking. I said yes, and then he remembered that you came to his college about a year ago and were talking about breaking out of the man box."

Not long ago, I was in a town in the Midwest and was working with a organization that engages men to work with women to end domestic violence and sexual assault. I was coming out of my hotel and I noticed a bunch of guys sitting outside of the hotel. One of them said to me, "Hey, we know you." They all agreed. I asked what he meant, and they proceeded to tell me what professional football team they played for, and that I was the "man box guy." We all laughed and talked for a few minutes. They shared that they enjoyed the talk we had had that day. Some spoke about how they have changed some of their "not so good" behaviors as a result of that talk.

I spoke at a high school once, and a teacher called me a couple of months later to tell me that the boys had created a great big man box. They keep it in the gym and call each other out on man box behaviors all the time.

Those are just a few examples of connections I have made with men and boys. Just imagine if coaches and men who work with boys from all around the country got onboard—think of the impact.

We ask coaches and other men who spend time with our sons and boys to do this with a heart of love. When we bring these messages to men wrapped in love it opens them up, even when their initial response is to shut down. Again, we bring it with love and whether or not men are interested in making an immediate change in their life. What becomes important is that because men are open and digest the information, they can't pretend they don't at least intellectually understand what is happening. Once we know, we know. We are no longer on remote control. We're making conscious choices now. Whichever way you decide to go, left, right, or whatever, you are doing it consciously. Coaches can play a major role in helping us reach our sons and other boys. Coaches can effectively help to get our sons and other boys off remote control, become more critical in their thinking, and no longer solely rely on tradition to guide them. Aid our sons and other boys in becoming leaders in the engagement of healthy respectful manhood.

If a man assaults his wife he goes to family court.

If he assaults a woman other than his wife he goes to criminal court.

The Hard Facts
It's Time to Get Outraged

Let's be clear, as stated earlier, men's violence against women is one of the leading causes of injury to women in our country. It is right up there alongside cancer and heart disease. The truth is most men are not aware of this. Most men have no idea of all the precautions women are taught to take in order to live in a society with us, men. Women are taught not to park next to vans for the fear of being pulled in when entering their car, with the van serving as a shield. Women are taught to park under a light when they go shopping or out to eat if they know it's going to be dark when they leave. They are taught to travel in groups of at least two, not alone. Women are taught to be careful when entering elevators or staircases. Women are taught to not stay at roadside motels alone. Other examples of precaution are: Don't jog alone when it's too early, or too late. Don't wear that dress, it's too revealing. Don't finish a drink if you left it unsupervised.

As you know, I grew up in New York City. I remember my mother telling my sister to always have her keys ready when she came into the building so she could enter the apartment quickly and could use the key as a weapon if needed. She had a saying for my sister, "Remember if you're looking for your keys, you're looking for trouble." When I think about this saying my mother would tell my sister, I know she used it to help her remember danger. But the part that said, "You're looking for trouble" is an example of how we as a society shift the responsibility of the violence from the offender (the man) to the victim (the woman).

In addition to all the things we tell women not to do, we have just as long a list of things we ask them to explain that begins with, "Why did you?" If she is attacked by a man we will want to know: Why were you out so late? Why did you wear that tank top? Why did you have so many drinks? Why didn't you leave with your girlfriends? One of the unfortunately classic statements with domestic violence is, "Why don't you just leave?" and then we say, "If she doesn't leave she must like it."

All of these statements are examples of what we call victim-blaming. These are examples of the ways in which we continue to hold women responsible for the behavior of men. Instead of constantly saying, "Why doesn't she leave?" what if the constant message was, "Why doesn't he stop?"

This reality speaks to how tough it is to get men interested in this subject because to do so would shake up the current construct of manhood. We are pushing the envelope when we de-construct the man box. We are challenging men to look and dig deeper into themselves and their beliefs. But that process is uncomfortable for men, and it's anxiety-provoking. This is not something that we just automatically decide is important. And it's not hard to see why.

Men aren't in the habit of looking at themselves in a group context and saying, "Well, while I am a good man, I am still part of this collective of men and this is what we do that is inappropriate to women." No, most men are taught to operate from a place of, "I am a good man and I don't do or support the behaviors of abusive men."

What this reality misses, though, is that all men, as part of the dominating group, consciously or subconsciously play a role in that system and institution of domination. It's like when white people say, "I am not racist; I know other white people are, but I am not." Many times that statement does not create the space to have the needed critical conversations about systematic institutional racial oppression. When whites refuse to self-reflect, or examine their relationship with other white people in the context of a race construct, they limit their ability to understand systematic institutional racial oppression. You can look at almost any dominating group in our country and come up with the same analogies.

So with this issue of why are we not outraged as men about violence against women and girls, one of the ways we can start this conversation is by acknowledging the reality that as men, for the most part, we have never been taught how to even discuss this or any of these conversations with each other. Most of us would not know, at least in an appropriate way, how to address the issues described in this book with each other, especially to talk about the subtle aspects of our behaviors that support or lead up to violence. When I speak with men about these issues, for most men, it's the first time they have been in such a gathering—either privately or publicly—with men having this discussion. It explains why it is so important for us to bring the conversation to men wrapped in love; their anxiety is usually just a step away from becoming very defensive.

Here's my experience: I've spoken with thousands of men, sometimes it's successful and sometimes not. If a man calls a woman the b-word in front of me, for instance, I might begin with, "You know, I hear what you're trying to say, but I want to share something with you. I get the sense that you are the kind of guy that would appreciate what I'm about to say. I want you to think about the kind of language you're using. What would be your thoughts if a man called your mother that? What would be your thoughts if your daughter came home and said one of the boys in the classroom called her that? What would be the feeling that would come up for you? How would that challenge you? I want you to think about that."

See, I don't go at men with, "What you said is wrong and don't do it again" or some threatening type of attitude. That's the wrong approach. A man shuts down when he hears that, and he immediately gets defensive. My tactic is simply to ask him to think about it. I'm not telling him to do anything. I just say, "I want to share with you. I think you would want to know this. I think you would want me to tell you this." I'm not pacifying him, but I'm trying to keep his defenses down as I initiate the conversation so that when I get to the heart of what I want to say to him, he hasn't already closed up and shut me out.

Generally, the reaction is along the lines of, "Yeah man, I hear what you're saying. I hear that." That sometimes is out of respect for me, and no more, and they may or may not be processing it.

Some men may say, "I hear you *but . . .* " And that means, I heard what you said. I appreciate what you said. But this is where I'm at. I'm not where you're at.

And some men are just more open to this line of thinking and say something like, "You know man, I never thought about it that way. I really appreciate you saying that. I'm not going to do that no more. It never dawned on me the wrong I was doing."

So I get the whole gamut, but what remains constant is my approach. In my experience, how you come to men is usually how they come back to you, not always but usually. The majority of the time even if they disagree with what I'm saying, because my position was stated with love, their response to me is also stated with love. Now, they might go somewhere else and say to one of their friends, "You know this jerk came up to me at school the other day after I called Kathy a bitch and tried to tell me how to talk!" That might be how they would describe it with someone else. I can't be sure of that, it's likely to happen. But the conversation with me is usually a loving conversation. And hopefully when they bring it to their friends or someone they respect, my position might actually get supported.

The one place I hear sharp disagreement with many of my teachings about the man box is on Internet sites where a TED Talk I gave in 2010, "Breaking Out of the Man Box," continues to make the rounds. I can go online and find fifteen different blogs with people chatting having just viewed it, and there you will hear some men upset about their place in a society promoting equal rights for women. They hardly if ever say anything about me personally. But online, they'll write things like, "I don't agree with this guy at all!" "This is bullshit; women are the problem not men" and so on. And they'll get into disagreements with women and other men—people are very comfortable sharing their true beliefs and feelings from the safety of their homes.

But even when I'm reading those kinds of messages where people are going back and forth at each other, the arguments are rarely based on the way I said what I said in the TED Talk. Rarely do I read people coming back at me and writing, "This guy is rude, and disrespectful of men." What I do read is people debating about or defining what they've gotten from my message. This is important to me as I try to sharpen my delivery of this information. I'm always looking for angles to reach in and grab the hearts and attention of men, which is not always an easy task. Many of the responses by men in these chat rooms help to remind and motivate me of the continued importance of this work. I'm putting it lightly when I say that some of the men's responses at times to women and other men are challenging, to say the least.

The most disrespectful responses are usually leveled at women. While it's challenging for many men to hear this information from men, it's even more difficult to hear them from women. What we have to keep in mind is that we are socialized to have less value in women, so the mentality is usually, *how dare she confront me on this or anything else*. So a woman may say the same thing that I did, and be equally or even more respectful in doing so, but men by and large will hear it "better" from me, the man. This not simply a bad guy, good guy conversation—this happens with most men in many situations; we outlined a few earlier in man box stories. Good guys are just as sexist as other men; no man gets a pass on this.

A man, a good guy, could have a hole in his wall at home that needs to be patched up. His wife can come in the room, look at the hole, and say, "There's this new product out that I saw, it would work great to patch up that hole." Now the man, a good guy, while hearing his wife is saying to himself, *I'm going to use what I use, how I use it. I know how to patch up a hole!*

But some random guy could come in, see the hole in the wall, and say, "You know what, I see you've got that hole in your wall. There's this new product out . . ." And if we are honest as men we might give him our undivided attention, take the time to listen to him, and even investigate the product he is referring to. The woman might know ten times more about patching a hole than the man does, but because he's a man, he will get our attention in a way she won't. It might feel like a stretch to some men, but this type of thinking defined by our collective socialization requires us to have less value in women.

Even men who have been studying these issues we are talking about, and practicing living as equals, will slide back at times into the man box. The difference between them and maybe other men is that they are no longer on remote control. They're not just simply doing things as they have always done them. These men actually know what they're doing, when doing it. It's not that men of a higher consciousness have it all together, granted they are working on themselves and moving in a positive direction. What also comes with this self-awareness is that they know when they're tuning women out and should be listening. Whereas another man who might not be as conscious of his behavior may not even realize what he is doing, men of higher consciousness know for the most part exactly what they're doing; whether it's right or wrong, they know when they are firmly out of the man box, as well as when they are entrenched in it. I understand this well, I'm one of those men. As men we are all in this together.

The question is not whether or not men are sexist. It's whether or not we know that we are, and whether or not we're trying to be better. Being anti-sexist includes the process of putting intervals of time between your last sexist behaviors or getting a gut reaction when you know you're doing or saying something inappropriate. Also, the ability to challenge and check yourself is important, and not to rely on someone else (in this case particularly women) to let you know your behavior was inappropriate.

It also means remaining open to constructive criticism when it's given. Understand that it's not always about your intentions but more importantly the impact you had on someone.

Anti-sexist men need to change the language they use knowing that it can be extremely oppressive. There's a word that one might use that they used all the time, and then one day the word comes to my mind and you suddenly think, *Man, I don't like that word. Something about that word doesn't fit. You know what? I'm going to find another word to use. I'm not using that word anymore.* These are all examples, along with many more, that are part of the process of being an anti-sexist man.

THE COLLEGE CAMPUS ISSUE

College campuses today are a dangerous place for women. When you couple manhood that teaches less value and objectification with a pack mentality, it becomes a very dangerous place for young women. You couple that with the fact that many of our colleges are surrounded by drinking establishments. Far too many of our colleges have liberal alcohol policies. Far too often, our children are choosing colleges not only for the academic experience but how liberal the policies are in support of social life and partying.

At many colleges, because they don't have enough dorm space, the property surrounding the college has become rental property. The two houses next to where I previously resided in New York became rental property; I lived in a college town. There were twenty to thirty young people there all the time, with no rules or adult guidance. Heavy drinking was the norm, and with that comes high incidents of sexual assaults, including rape. My situation was similar to most; I didn't want to reside next to a college party house. So what do I do? I either sell my house to someone who wants to create a rental property, or I turn it into a rental property myself. Then what happens? The whole block becomes rental property for the college. Now we have numerous young people living on their own with limited to no guidance. The collective socialization that has taught men that women are of less value, are property and objects, particularly sexual objects, thrives off this dynamic.

Furthermore we have numerous fraternity houses around many of our colleges and universities. Many fraternities have been removed from campuses because of their refusal to follow rules. The problem I see with this is they simply move the fraternity house across the street from the campus. Unless you know the boundaries of the campus, you might not even know they technically are off campus. And now—because they're off campus—there are fewer rules around their behavior, parties, and curfews. Then you connect alcohol, peer pressure to the norms we have associated with manhood, and multiply it by twenty-five young men creating this pack-like mentality. There's no question that's why one out of four women will be sexually assaulted during her college stay. College and university campuses are very dangerous places for our daughters. It should also be mentioned that numerous young men and women come home from college with alcohol problems, having rarely or never drank alcohol prior to college.

What's happening on our college and university campuses contributes to why 75 percent of women who are raped are twenty-five years old and younger. All of this really begins to make a lot more sense. Why are we not outraged? How can our socialization as men leave us without any purposeful interest in ending this reality?

In addition, almost every college and university receives some type of federal funding. One of the things I would like to see happen is stiffer requirements related to sexual assault prevention for colleges and universities seeking federal funding. All federally funded colleges and universities should be required to have prevention education, sexual assault awareness programs, and appropriate consequences for offenders that are tied to policy. All federally funded colleges and universities should be required to have services designated to support women and men who have been victims of sexual assault.

I would like to go a step further and say that every college and university should have a women's center. I would also like to see every college and university have initiatives focused on men, and healthy, respectful, and loving manhood. Creating mandates such as these for those receiving federal dollars could have a huge impact in our quest to lower and eliminate incidents of sexual assault on college and university campuses. What I am saying is not rocket science—it is basic common sense, but as long as we as men have a limited interest in the experience of women and girls, it might as well be astrophysics.

We must address our history of women as the property of men, while we know it's technically no longer true, it's very much tolerated still today in many of our communities and laws. Still today if a man assaults his wife he goes to family court. If he assaults a woman other than his wife he goes to criminal court. Obviously criminal court has stiffer consequences than family court. So what is the message here? Are we saying that if a man hits his wife he should have less accountability than if he hits a stranger?

The majority of men are just trying to hold it down and do the right thing. The majority of men are loving and kind men. There is a real issue that good men have to struggle with, a question that has to be answered and then a resolution applied. The question is: How is it that such a minority of men get to abuse women to the degree of epidemic proportions in the presence of a majority of good men? In the presence of good men does not mean they were there when the violence happened, but it does mean that it's happening, as men would say, on our watch.

Good men have to critically examine their relationship with men who are abusive: What are our similarities as men? What are the differences? And how might good men be benefitting from abusive men's behaviors? A fair question to ask is while good men would never abuse women, do they still have more in common with abusive men than differences? Are good men part of the problem or the solution? If women could have ended the violence on their own they would have. If the majority of men really took this issue on we could have a major impact on our quest to end violence against women and girls. It's time to get outraged.

Men change when they become more uncomfortable than comfortable with their old behaviors.

In the Midst of It All, I Believe in Men

With work, patience, and courage, a man can spend more time outside the man box than in it. The first, most important step for any man is to surround yourself with like-minded men who are thinking the same way. It's not going to be perfect. Any man new to examining himself on issues of equality has to understand that it's a long, uncomfortable but rewarding journey. So he'll need to find many things at different times to motivate him to stay on track. A lot of what motivates me is the world I want to see for my daughters and the kind of men I want my sons to be. Like with most things, it helps me to get outside of myself to see the bigger picture. I encourage men to do that, as well.

One of the things that I help men change is the discomfort of knowledge. Having new information, knowing the right thing but remaining the same is challenging for men. If you can, first, get a man on this journey. Then second, get him to spend some critical and purposeful time focused on the deconstruction of the man box, and things will happen—change will come. What I have seen is that men become excited about being on this journey, like any other newfound thing. That doesn't necessarily change men to the degree that we would want to see men change, though. I think what changes men is when they become more uncomfortable than comfortable with their old behaviors.

For example, as stated earlier, when a man is with a group of his friends and hears one of them disrespecting a woman, he may say nothing, just simply remain quiet. One of the reasons he stays quiet is because he doesn't want to offend his friend who's being disrespectful. Another reason he may remain quiet is because he instinctively knows that it's wrong to participate. He is uncomfortable sharing in the disrespect and that is what keeps him quiet. But the action we want to see from men is for them to be so uncomfortable remaining quiet that it motivates them to do something or say something. We want to increase the discomfort in men so much that they can't just be quiet; they have to tell the other guy to stop. The extreme discomfort is what will move men to action. But men don't feel uncomfortable enough to take action until they begin examining all these man-box issues in their own lives.

For me, when I hear a man say something inappropriate to a woman, I feel uncomfortable letting him walk away and then saying to the woman afterwards, "Oh, I heard what he said. I'm sorry he said that." Just the thought of that is extremely uncomfortable for me. What's become the better option for me is challenging his behavior (wrapped in love) in front of the woman. I have come to know within myself that it would be more uncomfortable for me looking at her afterwards (having said nothing) than it would be speaking up on her behalf. It must be noted that

I have not always been this way; this is simply part of my journey. I must also say that I don't do this every time the opportunity shows itself. There are times when I have remained silent and should have said something; I may have been afraid for many reasons or unwilling to possibly hurt the man's feelings, or just not in the mood for challenging anyone. This is not about perfection, it's about starting your own personal journey in becoming an anti-sexist man.

Not every man will want to do this, though. For one thing, it requires men on a daily basis to work at staying outside of the man box. When the reality is, whether we admit it or not, as men we enjoy domination. It might sound cruel but it's true; we enjoy power and also control. We don't necessarily enjoy doing bad things, but we marvel in the privileges that come with being a man. As men for the most part we find comfort inside the man box. Actually one of the goals of my work is to make living inside the man box uncomfortable. Another way to say it is that living outside the man box is also promoting equality for women and girls.

When women speak about equality, often men's concern is, "What am I going to have to give up?" Men, whether they openly say it or not, are concerned with what they may have to lose in support of making equality happen. The goal is to assist men in seeing the gift of equality. So instead we want men to see what they are gaining by supporting equality, instead of what they are losing.

Men, like any other dominating group (white people, financially wealthy people, heterosexual people, able-bodied people), for the most part are socialized to only see what they're losing—namely dominance and privilege, though at the same time they would not refer to it as such. Dominant groups are more likely to speak about privilege in terms of what they have earned through their own merit. In society, when we speak of equality it most always appears to members of dominating groups that the marginalized group is seeking something without earning it. As mentioned earlier, dominating groups rarely look at institutional and systematic forms of group oppression, everything has the appearance to them that it's based on meritocracy.

What's most important is that far too often dominating groups don't seem to realize how much humanity they have to gain. Men unfortunately have not been socialized to see and experience the beauty of humanity in respect to women in general. Now where that differs is when a man looks into the eyes of his daughter for the first time, his "baby girl." At that moment the world begins to shift for him, what he wants for her may quickly become more than what he is willing to give to a society of women himself. This is the conflict that men with daughters experience on a regular basis. A great question for men with daughters is to ask themselves, "Would I want my daughter to marry me?"

So the equality that we are hoping for, working with men and women, is a loving experience. It's holistic and liberating, removing the barriers that are between us as people. I know for some men that doesn't sound appealing and, based on our collective socialization, it might not be, but we have to come to terms with the reality that many aspects of the man box are destroying us all. When we think honestly and critically about this, there are not too many instances where this isn't true.

Whether you're a young man who is into hip-hop or an older guy still humming Motown, the work is still the same. With the many demographical differences among men, male domination over women looks more alike across cultural groups than different. This movement is not intended to take away from men— we should have pride in the many wonderful things that have been passed down from generation to generation. Most men are taught to be hard working, providers, loving husbands, partners, and fathers. While at the same time there are some aspects of manhood that we collectively have to rethink and challenge.

Be it geography or culture, you're going to have different norms and experiences with men. Whether men are financially poor or wealthy will have its own set of dynamics as well. Be it white men versus men of color, a younger man versus an older man, a man born in the United States, a man born outside the United States, a Christian man, a Muslim man—you're going to have those kinds of dynamics but within each group, men are socialized to see less value in women. In each group, men are taught to view women as the property of men. One group might be more extreme than the other, but it's still taught in each group. In each group, men are taught that women are objects, particularly sexual objects, and when you look at the three as an equation: Less value plus property plus objectification will always equal violence against women and girls. That same equation plays out all over the world.

Hopefully, the information and perspective of the previous chapters have helped you to understand, accept, and own some of our issues as men. Sexism continues to be at the root of violence against women and girls. This aggressive and dominating nature of men with regard to women can be seen in our history, traditions, and accepted socialization. Men often feel a sense of entitlement due to male privilege and advantages that gender provides. Unfortunately, our cultural norms support this belief that women have less value than men and that the role of women is to comfort, please, and entertain men. Being overtly and covertly demeaning, oppressive, controlling, and displaying abusive behavior toward women continues to be commonplace in our society. This social ill cannot be rectified without men first acknowledging and owning responsibility for it and becoming active in ending it. Well-meaning men cannot keep ignoring the problem that touches so many lives and has the potential to affect their loved ones at some point.

Not only are women the victims, but violence against women affects children, destroys families, and disrupts communities and places of work. First individually, and then collectively, well-meaning men must stand up and hold each other accountable. We are all responsible and can be change agents in ending violence against women and girls. For many years, the sexual and domestic violence movements, concerned citizens, activists, advocates, and many other dedicated people have been tremendous change agents and have made remarkable progress in the effort to create safety for women and accountability for men. Unfortunately, despite years of great effort, sacrifice, and loss of lives, the terror that women experience has not decreased.

Abusive men continue to get away with violence and intimidation as well as the misuse of many other forms of power for the purpose of controlling and dominating women. This is no reflection on the efforts of the women's movements or any other effort for social change. However, it is a reflection on well-meaning men and the lack of interest we have shown to these issues. This is especially disturbing because the pain, suffering, exploitation, and immeasurable loss that women experience is almost always due to violence and abuse at the hands of men. It's really time for good men to get educated, engaged, and involved.

Violence against women is a human rights violation. If any group were to attack another group of people who are law-abiding, peaceful, loving, and productive members of a society, the offending group would be in violation. But we absolve men of responsibility in the matter by calling violence against women a "women's issue" instead of a societal issue, or better yet a "men's issue." By categorizing domestic violence, rape, sexual assault, and other forms of violence against women as a "women's issue," we minimize the seriousness of the problem. Good men (the majority of men) are less likely to pay attention to the issue because they believe it does not have anything to do with them.

Moreover, often we label women who organize to fight oppression as special interest groups, minority groups, or feminists groups. These groups are underestimated and at times not taken seriously because of their lack of status, influence, resources, and perceived value. However, well-meaning men can learn a lot about men's abuse and the reality women experience every day by listening to what they have to say. We must all begin to use language that speaks to the issue of men's violence against women, which will aid in effectively holding men accountable. Often we use terms like relationship abuse, intimate partner violence, date rape, and other generic and neutral terms for fear of making men uncomfortable. But we need to call it what it is: men's violence against women, which names the major offender—men.

We do not need to protect men from their primary responsibility to deal directly with this issue. The focus has to move past women and their victimization to men and their perpetration of these crimes. Men choosing to remain silent when a woman is being abused reinforces abusive behavior. Our silence is also our permission if we decide to stay quiet; it is an act of collusion to protect male interests. Silence normalizes the abusive behavior that causes harm to women. I know that for most men it is not our intention to support men who are violent toward women. But we have to understand that our silence at the end of the day is permission. Abusive men are counting on us to remain silent, they are counting on good men to continue to support them by staying true to age-old notions of manhood. Abusive men are counting on good men to continue to view her as his property with an understanding that he can do with it as he chooses. Abusive men are counting on good men to continue to revictimize women who are sexually assaulted by questioning why she was there, or why she wore that dress when she should have known better.

There is no neutral position for men to take on this issue.

Violence against women is a problem that each man must own and make a personal commitment to end. It will not cease until we are collectively responsible. I ask all men to examine their own socialization and beliefs about women. Take ownership of the problem to create positive social change. Be honest, transparent, and willing to give up your privilege.

In addition, confront your man box issues, and the ways it supports men's domination, power, aggressiveness, and sexual objectification of women. Step out of the man box when raising your sons and be an example for all boys and men around you. Stop supporting strip clubs, men's magazines, and other outlets that degrade women. Do not make excuses for any type of abuse, whether it is verbal or physical, regardless if you know the people involved or not. Intervene or call the authorities when you witness violent behavior. Verbalize outrage in reference to violence against women, as well-meaning men have been silent too long. Galvanize other men, utilize your resources, and exert your influence within the community to create appropriate programs and interventions that address violent men.

Most importantly, listen to women. Their voice is important and we can learn a lot from them. If we do not start listening, the imbalance of power will endure. Women have been working to eradicate sexism for years; they have the knowledge, experience, and perspective we need. We must follow their leadership. After all, women are the experts on the violence and abuse men have perpetrated against them. They have a voice, but men have not been listening. We will not fully understand their oppression until we step out of the man box and sincerely receive the information.

When equipped with knowledge, we will make better decisions that are thoughtful and responsible. This is not about the need for women to have men save, protect, or rescue them.

Women don't need protection; they need men to stop being violent. As men who can be a part of the solution, this is about us being more involved. The reality is that when all men respect women as we should, safety will take care of itself and violence against women will decline and maybe someday end. The man box does not have to define well-meaning men forever.

Social change will require that we address our fears and anxiety while creating a new standard of behavior. Change can be tough for everybody; we need not fear as men how we will be perceived by others for taking on this issue of humanity. Or whether others may think we are soft or weak for ignoring the expectations of the man box in our collective socialization. Yet, we must understand that operating outside of the man box is the true sign of a real man because it takes a special courage and strength.

The moment men decide to fully own our responsibility for violence against women will be the moment we are on the road to social change. This will require integrity, accountability, and consistency through words and actions. We look forward to the day when the measurements of a true man do not depend on the threat of his words, the intimidation of his stature, the power in his eyes, the lust of his thoughts, or the violence in his fists. We believe the day is coming when manhood will be redefined. We are creating a world where all men and boys are loving and respectful and our daughters, mothers, sisters, wives, partners, and all women are valued and safe.

Ending violence against women and girls is primarily the responsibility of men.

The New Manhood Manifesto

Ted Bunch and I, along with the staff of A Call To Men, have been working across this country and many places globally for the past twenty years with the goal of eradicating sexism, while maintaining strong coalitions with women's organizations already doing this important work. We love working with communities in order to raise awareness and get men involved in ending violence against women and girls.

We truly believe ending violence against women and girls is primarily the responsibility of men. Although historically it has been almost entirely women who have been at the forefront addressing this issue, we think it is essential that men play a primary role in the solution to it. To do that, well-meaning men— men who, for the most part, don't see themselves as part of the problem have to get involved. These are seven guiding principles that men can take away from this book:

- **Male dominance does not exist.** Men's violence and discrimination against women and girls is rooted in a history of male domination that has deeply influenced the definition of manhood in our culture. This definition of manhood has three primary aspects that promote and support a culture of violence and discrimination against women and girls. It teaches that women are of less value than men, the property of men, and sexual objects.

- **It is men's work to end domestic and sexual violence against women**. Preventing domestic, sexual, and all forms of violence and discrimination against women and girls is primarily the responsibility of men. This also includes the promotion and teaching of the healthy concepts of manhood to each other, our sons, and other boys.

- **All forms of violence and discrimination need to be addressed.** We cannot focus only on one form of violence and discrimination against women and girls. All forms of violence and discrimination against women and girls are interwoven. We cannot end one form of violence without working to end them all.

- **Respect the voices of women in work and life.** While men are primarily responsible for ending men's violence, this cannot be done without adhering to the voices, leadership, and experiences of women. When working to end any form of abuse you must be accountable to those experiencing the abuse.

- **Be aware of intersections of oppression.** We have to be purposeful and comprehensive in our work, understanding that many women and communities experience multiple forms of oppression. Without this understanding our work will be limited and "mainstream focused." This approach is required if our work is to end violence against all women. It also then requires us to work with all men.

- **Commit to grassroots community-based efforts.** Ending violence against all women and girls requires collaborative efforts with grassroots culturally specific (and otherwise) community-based organizations. These organizations have to be part of (and in many respects lead) the process if we are to engage in any purposefully cultural-specific prevention efforts.

- **Continue hope for men.** The majority of men don't perpetrate violence against women and girls, what they are responsible for is creating, maintaining, and benefiting from a male-dominating culture that's required for the violence to exist. Once educated to these realities we believe there is hope for men.

By strategizing with groups across the United States, our vision at A Call To Men is to shift social norms that define manhood in our culture, and produce a national movement of men committed to ending violence against women and girls. A Call To Men is unique in its ability to be affirming and respectful to the experiences of women while expressing genuine care and hope for men.

Please join us.

Afterword

By Ted Bunch, cofounder of A Call To Men

Tony Porter approached me almost twenty years ago with the idea of talking to men about ending violence against women and girls. We both recognized that the solution to the problem of domestic violence, sexual assault, sex trafficking, and all forms of violence against women was the involvement of men. At the time, I was running the largest program for domestic violence offenders in the country. My program saw about six hundred men a week, all of whom were court mandated to attend a batterers intervention program for twenty-six weeks. Tony and I were part of a national training team that went around the country speaking about the role of batterer programs and different types of batterer interventions. We immediately became friends and began to develop the analysis for what would become the foundation of the work we do at A Call To Men. At that time we were learning from women who had been on the front lines of ending violence against women and eradicating sexism for years. Two of those leaders who were most influential in our development were Gwen Wright, executive director of the NYS Office for the Prevention of Domestic Violence, and Phyllis Frank, associate executive director of VCS Inc. Prior to our work in domestic violence, Tony and I both worked in the field of chemical dependency. We were both administrators and clinicians. As part of my work as a clinician I developed and implemented programming for chronic relapsing male clients. This population of men was not able to stop their drug or alcohol use despite many attempts at treatments of inpatient and/or outpatient therapies. They couldn't establish any significant recovery, they would try and they would fail.

Many people who become dependent on alcohol or drugs often seek to escape through the substances, as a way to medicate themselves from the pain or problems in their lives. The substances provide a temporary sense of well-being and a false sense of hope or perhaps courage. In my experience, most men who I counseled in treatment were covering up or medicating the pain from their lives or childhood, or their inability to express their emotions in a healthy way. Much of that pain can be tied directly to how they were raised as boys and taught to be men. For example, they were not able to cry or openly express feelings and constantly had to demonstrate that they were tough and not afraid. They were raised like almost every boy in our society, needing to prove every day in some way, form, or fashion that they were not weak and had no fear.

Through my work with this population of men I became recognized in the New York City area as someone who specialized in working with challenging populations of men. In 1994, I was recruited to run a domestic violence men's batterers program for Safe Horizon (formerly Victim Services). While directing the batterers program, which was educational and accountability centered, I utilized a political analysis from the battered women's movement. That perspective was that men's violence against women was rooted in the patriarchal structure of our society that encourages and teaches men to be sexist and believe that they are superior to women.

The belief that domestic violence is rooted in a patriarchal society was not a popular stance in the '90s. The models of "intervention" at the time by most programs and court systems sought to pathologize the violence of men and find other reasons for their behaviors. The issue of masculinity, manhood, and male socialization has always been of interest to me. I was raised as a pro-feminist by parents who were civil rights activists. I was invested in educating men about sexism and oppression and not pathologizing the violence. We wanted to be very clear that men's violence against women was a choice rooted in a patriarchy. This was fairly radical in those days. The notion of challenging the entitlements and privileges of men scared folks and still does.

Many approaches for "batterer intervention" were either a form of anger management or mental health treatment. While some people who are violent are also mentally ill, that was not the population that was coming through the batterer program I ran, which I almost immediately renamed the Domestic Violence Accountability Program (DVAP). The nearly 1,800 men a year who were being referred to DVAP were all mandated through the court. These men did know how to be respectful, nonviolent, and appropriate. They demonstrated that ability and control over their words and actions in their daily lives. They did not hit their boss or the police or anyone other than their wife or girlfriend. If their violence and abuse was due to mental illness it would show up everywhere, not just with women. Mental illness is not selective or exclusive, but male violence is.

In my early days as the director of DVAP, I remember going on a domestic violence call with two courageous and dedicated NYPD police officers in the Bronx. The 911 call brought us to a two-story walk-up on Tremont Avenue. As we went into the building we heard a man's voice; he was yelling, screaming, and making all kinds of threatening and degrading statements to whom we later learned was his wife. We heard what sounded like a person or objects being thrown against the walls. It was awful. As we approached the door, it was very loud and the police officer knocked on the door and said, "This is the police! Open the door!" Immediately, it became quiet. You could hear a pin drop and the man opened the door and very calmly said, "Hello, officers. May I help you?"

At that moment, as angry as he may have been, he was able to manage his anger just fine. So, it was not in any way about an inability to control himself or his temper. It was about him being the boss, in control, and demonstrating that power any way he chose. When there is a consequence, men almost always manage their anger. Even when a man is drinking and intoxicated and he's abusive with his intimate partner, when the police show up, he's still intoxicated, but somehow he knows to stop swinging. He knows whom he can hit and whom he can't hit. The belief system actually overrides the intoxication. That belief system begins as soon as we put the blue blanket on the baby boy leaving the hospital. That is the belief system that teaches our sons and other boys almost immediately that girls are of less value than boys.

As Tony and I began to spend more time together as part of a national training team and learning from the incredible women who were leading the way, we began to have conversations about the bigger picture. We decided that if it is about a patriarchy, if it is about male domination, if it is about sexism, then it must be about *all* men and, therefore, we do not need to focus our attention on such a small population of men who happen to get caught for perpetrating the violence, but on men as a whole. Of course, we believed individual men who were violent and abusive ought to be held accountable. However, it was clear that the actions of the individual men were in the context of male domination and the oppression of women, which is about men as a collective and that is what needed to be our focus.

At that time, the response to domestic violence was primarily focused on the efforts through the criminal-legal system, which reacts to the violence after it has occurred and not always in a fair or just way. Arresting offenders, just like building shelters for victims, is a response to the violence after the fact, a type of intervention. The work of A Call To Men was to go upstream and stop the violence from *ever* occurring. We knew that our calling was in prevention. We wanted to take the nonabusive men off the sidelines and get them involved. At first our work began as bystander intervention and then evolved to address the issue of manhood and masculinity.

One of the things that separates A Call To Men from most other men's organizations is our active investment in working with *all* men, no matter their history or what stage they're at in life. We work with boys, the elderly, professional athletes, fathers, teens, incarcerated men, etc. Wherever men and boys are, is where we want to be. We seek to go from the barbershop to the boardroom. You will find us in all circles.

Finding resources and support for the work of prevention has always been a challenge. Early on, we had a hard time finding funding for our work. We have always been very respectful of the space that we held in the Battered Women's Movements. Many were skeptical of a "men's" organization and for good reason. Among those reasons was the concern that men would do what men tend to do which is attempt to take over, and not take women, their voices, or concerns seriously. At that time, in the not-for-profit world of domestic violence and sexual assault there were only a handful of funders who were offering support. As a men's organization we did not want to, in any way, give the appearance that we were attempting to tap into funding streams that historically supported victim services. We never wanted to go after any of those resources. Not because the funders wouldn't have given it to us, but we didn't want to appear to be taking anything away from women or services for victims.

For the first three or four years, Tony and I supported the organization out of our own pockets. We both had full-time jobs and wives who believed in our work and us. We gave the cost of supporting the organization very little thought. We just focused on what we knew our work to be and spreading our message. Before you knew it, in less than two years, our work received national recognition and we began to lead the way in educating men about preventing men's violence against women. A few years passed and the field began to move more toward engaging men, we received more support from the advocate community, and some small funding opportunities began to come our way.

I believe that our work helped move "the movement" to embrace the work with men, and that only occurred because we were truly in solidarity with women and women's organizations. We were fortunate to understand our role and how to be accountable to the Women's Movement. We consistently demonstrated that we were allies and had women's backs. This helped us receive recognition, approval, and acceptance from the domestic violence and sexual assault movements; both have been great contributors to any success of A Call To Men.

In the beginning, working with women's organizations was where we spent much of our time. Domestic violence and sexual assault advocates were doing the heavy lifting as it relates to safety and fairness for women and girls. There were very few other men's groups doing significant national work. We knew that in order to do our work in an accountable, responsible, and ethical way, we wanted to be in solidarity with women's organizations. Building our work alongside of women really helped us to understand an in-depth analysis of feminism, how we as men impact women. We began to understand how to best work in ways that really provided support and affirmed the experiences of women while also providing hope and care for men.

In fact, more often than not, it is still women who bring us into their community to talk to the men. Women are doing the majority of important work to end violence against women and girls in their communities. It's also women who recognize, as we do, that men are the solution to men's violence.

In our work at A Call To Men, we have found that men respond well to storytelling and transparency. I remember sharing a story with a group of men about my daughter Maya, who graduated from college a few years ago. While attending school at the University of Virginia, in her last year she wanted to live off campus in Charlottesville, Virginia. Charlottesville is a college town, not much different than any other college town, and just as safe or just as dangerous, depending on how you look at it.

Her mother and I live in New York, about a six-hour drive door to door. We went down to see the apartment and met the two other young women that Maya was going to share the apartment with. The apartment was fine, and her mom and I approved. Then we went back to New York. Before I drove back down to Charlottesville to move Maya's things from home, she asked me to bring her an old pair of my shoes or boots. Now, men, why would she need a pair of my old shoes or boots? What purpose would the item serve? When I asked this question to the group of men, they answered, "She wants to put them outside her door. She wants to give the impression that a man is there."

"Why would she want to give an impression that a man was there?" I reply. A number of men then say, "So she feels protected, less at risk, and safe."

Now I have their attention. The next question is, "Who here has daughters, younger sisters, a niece, or young girls in your life that you care about and want safe?" Most hands will go up. My next statement is, "My daughter is six hours away, and I can't protect my baby girl." I have to turn her over to the men in Charlottesville and pray that she will be safe. "How would that make you feel?" I ask. The men respond, "uncomfortable," "afraid for her," "I don't want her to go."

Thank God, Maya has never been physically harmed, or sexually harmed, but she knows intuitively what we know statistically, which is that one in three women will be victims of domestic violence or sexual assault in their lifetime. Then I will approach one of the men who raised his hand earlier and ask him the name and age of his daughter. He tells me her name is Jackie and she is ten years old. I then ask him, "Wouldn't it be wonderful if when Jackie goes away to college or leaves your home to live on her own she doesn't have to put shoes outside of her door?" Every man says yes! That is prevention. We want stop it before it ever happens and that begins and ends with men and how we raise our boys.

While 80 percent of the men are not going to do anything that will intentionally harm women, my daughter does not put the shoes outside her door there 20 percent of the time; she has to put the shoes out there 100 percent of the time because, from where she's standing, all men are a potential danger.

Women and girls have to do things every day to feel safe and less at risk of being a victim of men's violence. The national statistics inform us that three women are killed every day by a current or former partner. Domestic violence and sexual assault are leading causes of injury to women in this country. In the United States 35 percent of all emergency room visits for women every day are directly or indirectly a result of men's violence. We also know that a minority of men inflict this epidemic of violence. Somewhere between 15 and 20 percent of men commit the acts of domestic violence, dating violence, and sexual assault. That means that almost eight out of ten men do not. We believe that if the eight say to the two knock it off, they will. Accountability from men to other men is the key. When the message to men who are abusive from men who are not abusive is that the harmful behavior will not be tolerated, then change will come about and the needed aspects of manhood will be redefined.

A neighbor in my community beat his wife badly in 2006. I lived on a block that had a cul-de-sac at the end. There's no through traffic and everyone knows everyone else. If someone came down the block who we didn't know and, for instance, parked his or her car, any neighbor would feel comfortable going to that person and asking, "May I help you?" It was really a close community in that way.

Well, two houses down from me was my neighbor, and we'll call him John. I came home one night, and the police and an ambulance were at John's house and the ambulance took his wife to the hospital. He had broken her nose and her cheekbone and the police had arrested John. He was released the next day and immediately came back home. His wife didn't return for a few more days from the hospital, so he was there alone. During that gap of time before John's wife came home, I felt compelled to do something, so I went and got two other men from our community and we went and paid John a visit.

Now, the men and I certainly could have done a number of things, but we went to John not to intimidate him, not to threaten him, but in love and in peace. We knocked on John's door and when he answered, we said, "Men in this community don't behave that way. You need to stop it. We hope you'll join us in that." Then we left and he closed the door. He didn't say, "Get off my step" or anything like that. He just closed the door. He actually had a look that I would describe as shame. I didn't see John for a day or so; the next time I saw him he was driving from the entrance of our block toward his home, which is a few houses past mine. In the past John would normally drive down the street past our house and wave to my wife and me like all the other neighbors. But this time, I could hardly see his head over the steering wheel.

As the days and weeks went by when I'd see him at the store, he would go the other way. I believe there was something that happened inside of John that really challenged him because a community of men had said, "This is not okay." Domestic violence has been seen as a private issue, and that privacy has always been for the benefit of men. That privacy is based again on women being perceived as the property of men. With that comes a belief system that states anything that happens in a man's house, he has responsibility for, control over, power over, even dominion over, some would say.

Fortunately, violence against women in the home or anywhere else is not a private issue but rather a public issue. Ideally what we'd like is a public response so when John goes to his workplace on Monday morning, men in that community would say to John, "We heard what happened and men who work here don't behave that way. We hope you'll join us and stop it." When he goes to his church, his mosque, his synagogue, his temple, men there say the same thing: "We love that you're here with us, John, but men who worship here don't behave that way. You need to stop it." When he goes to play golf with his friends and they get ready to tee off, they say, "John, this is the last game we can play with you if you do that again." That's what's going to change the mindset of men. That's what's going to change our culture. That's what's going to shift our social identity as men. Men's violence against women is an issue that men need to accept and own.

In the spirit of full disclosure, I had heard John yelling other times before, and I didn't do or say anything. I didn't say, "Hey man, I hear you having some challenges at home. Are you okay?"

Of course what most men would say is, "Yeah, I'm fine," because asking for help is viewed as a sign of weakness. It's almost as if because we're never supposed to not be okay, that's all a part of the teachings of the man box. I always regret not reaching out to him earlier. Perhaps that would have, in some small way, made him feel some sort of accountability when he decided to raise his hand to his wife. Or maybe he might have been able to come over to me to say he needed to talk. One man's voice might have made a difference.

Just as much as we are working to end men's violence against women, we're also invested in the well-being of men. There is a perception among some men that if you are supportive in some way toward women, that somehow equates to being against men. For many men it feels as if they are losing ground or being penalized for women to be seen as and treated equally to men. At A Call To Men we have never believed that to be true. A staple of our work, which Tony states at the end of his highly acclaimed TED Talk, is that "the liberation of men is directly tied to the liberation of women." We believe that violence against women is a human rights issue, and that it should be treated in that way, and that all people should be held with dignity and respect.

Fortunately, we have seen some shift in the collective beliefs, attitudes, and behaviors of men over the years. I'd like to think that the work of A Call To Men had something to with that. While there has been movement made around the issue of addressing sexism, patriarchy, male domination, and violence against women, there's also been a backlash from "men's rights groups," as if men don't have rights. "Men's rights groups"—that's a confusing term to me. It appears that some of these groups only seek to disempower and oppress women. This should not surprise us because as sexism and patriarchy are challenged, we can expect that sexism and patriarchy will rear their ugly heads with some sort of retaliation or backlash.

We see this with antiracism work as well. Like any form of group oppression or "ism," sexism operates the same way. When people seek liberation, those systems that are in place to suppress that liberation continue to oppress and find new, different, and more sophisticated covert and overt ways to do so. Case in point: In 2013 it was difficult to get the Violence Against Women Act reauthorized. This was because of those who objected to extending the act's protections to same-sex couples and to provisions allowing abused illegal immigrants to claim temporary visas. The Violence Against Women Act of 1994 (VAWA) is a United States federal law drafted by the office of Senator Joe Biden, signed by President Bill Clinton to provide much needed funding to those working on the behalf of ending violence against women. The Act also establishes the Office on Violence Against Women within the Department of Justice.

That doesn't make any sense at all, does it? You wouldn't think that there would be any question or debate about whether our country should be a safe place for women. You would think that there would be no question that there should be accountability and laws that support such basic rights in a civil society. Women still aren't getting the same wage for the same work as men even though one of the first things President Obama did after being elected was sign a law—The Lilly Ledbetter Fair Pay Act of 2009 to address this very issue. But it doesn't necessarily make a day-to-day difference. Theory and practice are two different things.

Over the years, the work, vision, and mission of A Call To Men has evolved. We began with a primary focus on bystander intervention and have grown to address all aspects of manhood. We recognize that in order to prevent violence and discrimination against women and girls, we must address how we define ourselves as men. New concepts of manhood and masculinity are needed. A more loving, healthy, and respectful manhood must be embraced. We recognize that as we increase and promote a loving, healthy, and respectful manhood, we decrease and prevent domestic violence, sexual assault, bullying, and homophobia. Those ills cannot exist with the evolved manhood that we want to create. Our vision is to create a world where all men and boys are loving and respectful and all women and girls are valued and safe.

It's imperative that we look to community leaders, organizers, and influencers as we educate, engage, and empower men to challenge and talk to other men. It is essential that we engage, respect, and recruit from this body of men in order to get more men from grass roots communities involved. We want to impact change with men from all demographics. The shortest distance between two points is a straight line; we want to work with men who have that direct line of communication with men.

On another note, my son, Josh, presented a great example of challenging the social and cultural norms that define manhood when he came to me with a question in the fall of 2011. Josh was a freshman in high school. He is a gifted athlete. He eats, sleeps, and drinks sports. If he is not playing a sport he is playing a sports video game on his Xbox or watching ESPN. One day in September, Josh came to me and asked to dye his socks pink. Pink . . . the most feminine of colors. Why pink? What was so special about pink for my son who spent much of his time in our society's hyper-masculine pursuits?

He wanted to wear his pink socks on the football field during practice and his games. He wanted to be like the men who he looked up to in the National Football League who were wearing pink during the month of October in recognition of Breast Cancer Awareness Month. Now, at that time, Josh was not interested in organizing a 5K for breast cancer or even learning about the disease. He was interested in being like the men who many other men, young and old, admire.

After football season Josh wore those pink socks and other pink socks during basketball the entire season for practice and games. He was able to purchase additional pink socks and other pink items for all sports he played at any sporting goods store that he went to because currently there is a billion-dollar market for pink sports apparel for men. Now, three years later, he wears many pink items of clothing. He has pink sneakers; his teammates have pink sneakers, socks, and jerseys. In this short span of time, we have made a cultural shift. Today, the most "feminine" of colors, pink, has become a "masculine" color. Simply because men who other men look up to have said it's okay and actually "manly" for men to wear pink. This culture shift was accomplished without even trying, an unintentional consequence of a brilliant awareness campaign. Imagine if we were intentional about making changes.

It's important that we examine social and cultural change as it relates to men's violence and discrimination against women and girls. We want men to view it as something personal to them, not just something to be done for the sake of women. Women do not need to be rescued or saved. What is needed is for men not to be violent and safety will take care of itself.

For example, if a man says something to a woman on the street that's offensive, we want other men to be offended by that. Imagine if the harassment was race based instead of gender based, if there's a white man who is walking down the street with his buddy, and his buddy (who is also white) yells out a racial slur to a black person they see. His friend would say to him, "Hey man, you can't do that!" "I'm surprised at you," or something like that. We need the same type of immediate reaction to happen when a man says something inappropriate to a woman, when it is gender based.

We are turning a corner as it relates to the social change efforts directed toward men about how we view and treat women. We are capable of creating social change very quickly. A wonderful model and example to follow is the creation of laws and education about alcohol and driving under the influence. Driving While Intoxicated (DWI) laws and response did not exist much twenty years ago. But today there is a clear and swift response by our legal system, by communities, by parents with their children, in school systems, procedures for purchasing alcohol have changed, the drinking age has gone up from eighteen to twenty-one. An entire national response was created around drinking and driving. Bartenders are being held accountable for serving intoxicated customers. Car insurance rates skyrocket for those with DWIs. Designated driver programs, ads, campaigns, etc., are commonplace. My children and I went out to dinner recently and as we were waiting to be seated at our table, my thirteen-year-old son Jalen sat on a stool at the bar and was asked not to because he was a minor. Not too long ago he could have ordered a Shirley Temple and nursed it all night. Everyone knows the rules of conduct as it relates to alcohol use and driving. This was all initiated by the extraordinary efforts of Mothers Against Drunk Driving.

Prior to the efforts of the movement to keep our roads and people safe, if someone had been drinking and was staggering to their car you would simply get out of the way. Even if he or she was pulled over there wasn't much of a consequence. And as bystanders, we would look at the intoxicated person and we would feel it wasn't our obligation or responsibility to do anything.

Now, if that same thing happens today, a person gets a DWI, his or her license is taken away, there is a financial penalty and probably a substance abuse program to attend. In other words, if they go to work and people know they got a DWI—it's no secret because a lot of people are in the newspaper who get DWIs or they're asking people for rides because they have a DWI and can't drive. There is embarrassment and even humiliation associated with receiving a DWI. Friends and family are going to be disappointed in your behavior, where twenty years ago there wasn't a harsh judgment on the behavior.

Now what accounts for the difference? Well, we as a society have put a lot of energy into laws about driving while intoxicated. You drive down the street and you'll see signs that read

"No drinking while driving." It'll tell you the consequence of drinking while driving. So much so that if somebody is in a store tonight, and you're walking down the street, and that person gets to their car staggering with a bottle and cheese, and you and only one other person, a total stranger, opposite culture, opposite gender, opposite religion, everybody, the most different person from you will look at each other and you will organize yourselves and you'll say, "We have to do something," because you will feel a sense of responsibility if you don't. That's social change.

We want that same thing to happen as it relates to violence against women and girls. That when it's seen, when it occurs, when it's exposed, we all have a social consciousness to do something about it. In order for that to happen we have to have an all-out, sustainable campaign, intense community responses, community organizing, legal sanctions, and expectations of behavior, so that we all know this is against the social contract of men in relationship to women.

We can also start raising our consciousness regarding what sexism is and how it gets played out. It's important as men that we become more aware of our own actions and attitudes about women, being transparent in our quest to make a difference. Transparency includes looking at ourselves as it relates to creating a world that's safe for women and girls. We can also support organizations that work toward ending violence against women and girls. And it is so important for us as men to support our boys doing things that are outside of the traditional social and cultural expectations of manhood.

We can be more open to functioning outside of the man box and its many aspects of hyper-masculinity. We have to develop an understanding that while aggression has its place in sports, in the military, and in the business world, in our personal lives we can actually be vulnerable, we can be open, we can support women to make decisions, and we can support women to provide leadership and vision. To do this, men have to get over our fear of being vulnerable. Masculinity, as it's defined by the man box, is so limiting and small. Understanding our full range of humanity means asking for help, letting people in, being vulnerable, not feeling like we have to be tough, not telling our boys to stop crying, talking about being sad when we're sad, having women as friends, those types of things. Understand that homophobia and heterosexism is the glue, the duct tape that holds the man box together.

Acknowledgments

I would like to express my gratitude to every individual who has trusted me enough to share their personal experiences. Also, to those who believed in this book and supported me, I also say thank you. Your insight and wisdom helped to make this journey possible.

I want to give honor to two very special women in my life. My journey to A Call To Men would have never happened without their love and mentorship: Phyllis Frank and Gwen Wright.

Very special thanks to my phenomenal wife, Tammy, whose love and devotion has created the space for me to do this work. Also, to my amazing children for keeping me humble and focused.

To my youngest son Kendell: We share a special relationship, which continues to help me grow as a father and a man. This book is full of "Kendell stories." Stories that I hope will help fathers to understand the important role they play in their sons' journeys to manhood.

To my spiritual advisors Reverend Marguerite Lee and Reverend Dr. Casey R. Kimbrough for reminding me how much I don't know. Helping me to remain teachable and trusting in God above all.

And last but surely not least to my dear friend and cofounder Ted Bunch; we have been traveling this journey called A Call To Men together for twenty years. Sharing in the joys and challenges, remaining committed to the work and each other. Thank you so much.